EAT

OUR

WORDS

RECIPES FROM
NEAR AND FAR

All Proceeds Go To
The Dugald McArthur Trust Fund

CHURCHILL LIVINGSTONE

EDINBURGH LONDON NEW YORK MADRID MELBOURNE SAN FRANCISCO AND TOKYO 1997

ISBN 0 443 061734

Eat Our Words was compiled, edited, designed and prepared for publication by the staff of Churchill Livingstone, Robert Stevenson House, 1-3 Baxter's Place, Leith Walk, Edinburgh EH1 3AF.

Copies of the book are available from Irene Ingram at the above address. Cheques should be made payable to *The Dugald McArthur Trust Fund*.

Preface

This recipe book is one of a number of initiatives being undertaken to raise funds for the Dugald McArthur Trust Fund. Dugald McArthur is a young man who, at 28 years of age, was severely injured in a rugby accident in October 1996. The accident has left him paralysed from the shoulders down and with only limited hand movement. His partner, Morven Meason, is a Production Editor with *Churchill Livingstone Publishers* in Edinburgh.

Most of the recipes in this book have been contributed by staff members of Churchill Livingstone in Edinburgh, London, New York and San Francisco along with a little help from their families and friends. We have also been very fortunate to receive recipes from professional chefs at some of the top restaurants and hotels in Edinburgh as can be seen from the Acknowledgements. The result is a remarkable selection - from cordon bleu to simplicity itself. We hope this mix of tasty recipes will provide a truly international flavour and the ideal opportunity to try something new.

No expenses have been incurred in the publishing and printing of this book. The design, page layouts, editing and production have been done by the staff of Churchill Livingstone. The artwork was done by Dugald's father, Bill McArthur, who is the political cartoonist with *The Herald* newspaper in Glasgow. We are very grateful to the suppliers listed in the Acknowledgements.

ALL the proceeds from sales will go directly to **The Dugald McArthur Trust Fund**.

Contributors

Robert Stevenson House, Edinburgh

Frances Affleck
Nancy Arnott
Pat Aubertel
Valerie Bain
Debra Barrie
Graham Birnie
Isobel Black
Alison Bowers
Caroline Boyd
Sarah Cape
Ann Collins
Kathy Crawford
Carol Curran
Ian Dick
Sheila Dickson
Amanda Dix
Lorraine Gibson
Deborah Gray
Claire Green
Ellen Green
Gillian Griffith
Ewan Halley
Stewart Hislop
Eileen Horne
Kay Hunston
Irene Ingram
Dilys Jones
Jim Killgore
Ailsa Laing
Inga Laurenson

Jane Lyness
Elspeth Masson
Katrina Mather
Clodagh McNamara
Douglas McNaughton
Suzanne McNeill
Morven Meason
Elizabeth Moreland
Barbara Muir
Ninette Premdas
Alan Palfreyman
Mike Parkinson
Douglas Pretsell
Gail Quinn
Robert Ramage
Sybil Ramsay
Elizabeth Reilly
John Richardson
Jan Ritchie
Derek Robertson
Margot Russell
Jane Shanks
Andrew Stevenson
Janice Urquhart
Marie Walmsley
Kate Walshaw
Gillian Watson
Jane Watson
Claire Wilson
Timothy Wright

Clerkenwell Road, London

Sarah Lowe

Gaye Turner

New York Office

Bridgett Dickinson

Bets Radley

Ann Ruzycka

vi

Acknowledgements

This project would not have been possible without the tremendous support of the following businesses:

Recipes

Caledonian Hotel, Edinburgh;

Giuliano's Ristorante, Edinburgh;

L'Auberge, Edinburgh;

Marriott Dalmahoy Hotel and Country Club, Edinburgh;

Restalrig Fruits, Edinburgh.

The recipe for stuffed marrow is reproduced from Alkmini Chaitow's *Recipes for Health - Arthritis* published by Thorsons/Harper Collins (ISBN 0722533179).

Film output

Syntax, 57 Timber Bush, Leith, Edinburgh EH6 6QH.

Production and Printing

Bell & Bain Ltd, 303 Burnfield Road, Thornliebank, Glasgow G46 7UQ.

Prontaprint, Edinburgh.

Paper

Paper Management Services Ltd;

Text Paper - G Print Matt 90gm^2 - Stora Fine Paper (UK) Ltd;

Cover Board - Fineblade Smooth Board 250 gm^2 - Hale Paper Co. Ltd.

Bookshops

Blackwells Bookshops at Ninewells Hospital, Dundee and Aberdeen Royal Infirmary, Aberdeen;

John Smith Booksellers, Strathclyde University Bookshop Branch, Glasgow;

James Thin Booksellers, South Bridge, Edinburgh.

Profile of Dugald

Dugald was born in Edinburgh's New Town in 1969, and spent his childhood years living on the island of Sanday in Orkney, with parents Bill and Sue, sister Samantha and brothers Liam, Fionn and Matthew. After leaving school, Dugald returned to Edinburgh and began a successful career in insurance with Scottish Provident. Always a keen sportsman, he enjoyed playing rugby for Broughton Rugby Club and was captaining his work's team for the first time when the accident occurred during a friendly match .

While making a tackle on another player, Dugald sustained an incomplete cervical spinal cord injury, level 4, in a whiplash action. The nerves at the base of his neck were damaged and compressed, causing the electrical impulses travelling from his brain to his body to become confused. This has led to loss of movement below his shoulders. His injury is defined as "incomplete" because there may be further improvements to his condition, and there have been many already.

The future for patients with spinal injury is optimistic, as a good deal of progress has been made in the past few years, especially in the field of rehabilitating damaged nerves and restoring the connection. The staff in the Queen Elizabeth Spinal Unit, Southern General Hospital, Glasgow have been remarkable in teaching Dugald to adapt and in helping him to deal with the limitations of his body.

Coping with the loss of limb movement must be one of the greatest challenges to face a young, fit person. Dugald has met these challenges with patience, hard work and, above all, good humour. His mind remains as sharp and clear as ever and his optimism seems to know no bounds. His inspiring top priority is to get back to work and return to the life in Edinburgh he enjoyed before the accident. But dealing simultaneously with the difficulty of accepting his disability and the desire to fight it makes day-to-day living a trial of strength.

The support Dugald has received from his friends and family has been tremendous. He feels fortunate to have so many people near him who are willing and wanting to be there for him. Dugald will not allow himself to indulge in self-pity and is determined that he will regain an independent lifestyle, one in which he can dictate his day-to-day living. Perhaps the real miracle which has emerged from this tragedy is the sheer will and determination that Dugald has found within himself in not allowing others to define him by his condition.

Morven Meason

Contents

EAT
OUR
WORDS

First Courses

When John Kennedy promised that by the end of the 1960s we would put a man on the moon everybody, including the scientists, shook their heads in dismay. But we did it. We can cure spinal-cord injuries too, if there's will. What was possible in outer space is possible in inner space.

Christopher Reeves

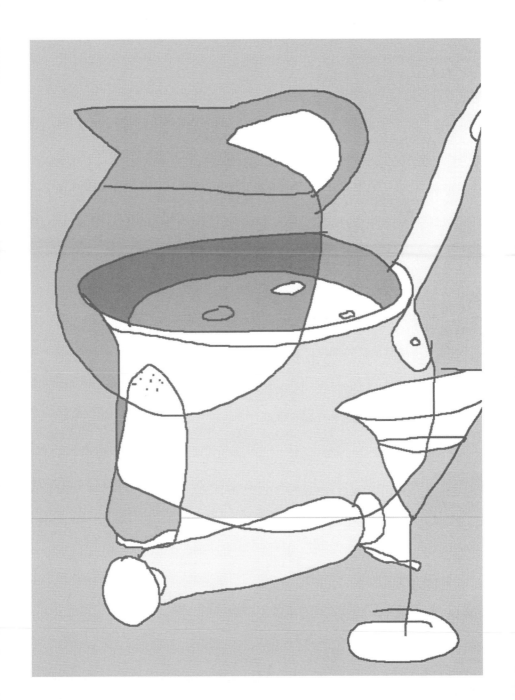

Cullen Skink

Traditional fish soup from the Moray Firth area of Scotland – very tasty!

Serves 4

Skin haddock fillets and place in a pan with just enough water to cover, bring to the boil and add onion. Reduce heat and simmer until cooked (5–10 minutes).

Prepare and cook potatoes. Mash well with a little butter. When fish is cooked, flake with a fork and add the milk.

Reheat, adding potato (quantity depends on thickness desired) and remaining butter to give a thick creamy consistency.

Serve very hot, garnished with parsley and serve with either oatcakes or wholemeal crusty bread.

6 smoked haddock fillets (kipper or smoked mackerel may also be used)
1 large onion, chopped
570ml (1 pint) milk
25–50g (1–2 oz) butter
salt and pepper
fresh parsley
225g (8oz) hot mashed potato

Prawn and Mint Soup

Leave cucumber for half an hour to drain.

Mix stock, tomato juice and yoghurt in food processor.

When mixture is smooth, stir in cucumber, garlic and cream.

Season and add prawns. Chill and stir in mint.

When serving, sprinkle with chopped egg.

1 large cucumber, peeled and diced
150ml ($^1/_4$ pint) strong chicken stock
150ml ($^1/_4$ pint) tomato juice
4 × 150g (5oz) pots natural yoghurt
150ml ($^1/_4$ pint) single cream
1 cup prawns, peeled and coarsely chopped
1 clove garlic, crushed
1–2 tbsp mint, chopped
1 hard-boiled egg
salt and pepper

Broccoli Soup

Courtesy of Restalrig Fruits.

Serves 4

175g (6oz) onions, sliced

175g (6oz) broccoli florets

25g (1oz) butter

3 level tbsp red lentils

845ml (1¹/₂ pints) chicken stock

Sauté onions and broccoli for 5 minutes on 'High' in microwave.

Stir in other ingredients.

Cover and cook for a further 10 minutes on 'High'.

Liquidize. Reheat for 2 minutes.

225g (8oz) cooked beetroot, peeled and cut into thin matchsticks

225g (8oz) potatoes, peeled and diced

225g (8oz) can tomatoes, sieved

225g (8oz) onions, finely chopped

2 rashers streaky bacon, finely chopped

1.14 litre (2 pints) chicken stock

2 tbsp vinegar

1 bay leaf

salt and pepper

150ml (¹/₄ pint) soured cream to serve (optional)

Borscht

Beetroot soup – popular in Poland, Russia and Ukraine. Borscht should be slightly piquant in flavour and not sweet. It is best 1 day old.

Serves 4–6

Cook onion and bacon gently in bacon's own fat until soft.

Pour over stock and vinegar and bring to the boil.

Add beetroot to stock and allow to simmer for approximately 5 minutes.

Add potatoes, tomatoes, bayleaf and salt and pepper to taste.

Simmer for 45 minutes.

Remove bay leaf before serving.

Soured cream is served separately.

Carrot and Orange Soup

Courtesy of Restalrig Fruits.

Serves 4

Put carrots, onion, butter, salt and pepper, sugar, bay leaf and stock in a covered dish and microwave for 15 minutes on 'High'.

Liquidize then add orange or lemon juice.

Reheat to serve.

450g (1lb) carrots, chopped
1 medium onion, chopped
40g (1¹/₂ oz) butter
salt and pepper
1 tsp sugar
1 bay leaf
845ml (1¹/₂ pints) chicken or vegetable stock
juice of two oranges or half a lemon

Carrot and Peanut Soup

Fry onions in oil until transparent. Add coriander, ginger, stock and carrots. Cook until soft.

Stir in peanut butter. Reheat to boiling point and then simmer for 5 minutes.

Keep stirring to prevent sticking at bottom of pan. Season to taste.

Just before serving, swirl in 1 dsp of soured cream and place a few hot garlic croutons on top.

2 medium-sized onions, finely chopped
1 tbsp oil
2 litres (3¹/₂ pints) stock (use chicken or ham stock cubes)
900g (2 lb) carrots, roughly chopped
110–165g (4–6oz) smooth or crunchy peanut butter
soured cream
1 rounded tsp coriander
1 rounded tsp ginger
garlic croutons
salt and pepper

Cauliflower Soup

Courtesy of Restalrig Fruits.

Serves 4

50g (2oz) butter

1 onion, finely chopped

2 tbsp plain flour

720ml (1¹/₄ pints) hot chicken stock

350g (12oz) cauliflower florets

salt and black pepper

2 tbsp single cream

1 tbsp parsley

Place butter and onions in a large bowl and microwave on 'High' for 2 minutes. Blend in flour. Gradually stir in stock and cook on 'High' for 2 minutes.

Place cauliflower florets in dish, cover and cook on 'High' for 7 minutes.

Add to sauce and cook on 'High' for 2 minutes. Liquidize then reheat.

Stir in cream and parsley before serving.

Cream of Tomato and Chicken Soup

900g (2lb) tomatoes, skinned and deseeded

1 large onion, chopped

2 sticks celery, chopped

2 carrots, grated

2 cloves garlic, crushed

1 can condensed chicken soup

¹/₄ tsp nutmeg

50g (2oz) butter

salt and pepper

Put butter into a large wok and sauté tomatoes and all vegetables for about 5 minutes.

Add chicken soup and a can of water and cook for about 10 minutes.

Liquidize the soup and transfer to a pan. Cook for about another 5 minutes.

Add salt, pepper and nutmeg.

Serve with crusty bread.

Garnish with fresh parsley and also a swirl of cream.

Cream of Mushroom Soup

Serves 4

Wash and roughly chop the mushrooms and their stalks.

Melt 25g (1oz) of butter in a large saucepan and add the chopped onion. Cook gently for 3 or 4 minutes until the onion is softened.

Add the mushrooms and the stock and simmer gently for 20 minutes with the lid on until the mushrooms have softened and reduced slightly. Allow the mushroom mixture to cool slightly for 10 minutes.

In a small saucepan, melt the rest of the butter and stir in the flour, cooking on a very low heat and stirring continuously for 1 minute until the mixture becomes a roux. Heat the jug of a liquidizer with warm water and place the roux in liquidizer. Add some of the mushroom mixture and blend for 30 seconds. Add remaining mixture, soy sauce and seasonings and blend for a further 30 seconds until mixture is smooth and creamy but still with a little texture.

Return to the saucepan and reheat gently.

Serve with a swirl of cream and a sprinkling of nutmeg.

350g (³/₄ lb) mushrooms (closed cup work well but use a variety if you want different flavour)

1 small onion, roughly chopped

425ml (³/₄ pint) vegetable stock (stock cube will do)

425ml (³/₄ pint) milk

75g (3oz) butter

50g (2oz) flour

salt and pepper

1 dsp soy sauce

Leek and Butter Bean Soup

450g (1lb) leeks, thinly sliced

150g (5oz) onions, finely chopped

1 tbsp oil

450g (1lb) can butter beans, rinsed

50g (2oz) smoked lean bacon, well grilled and cut into bite-sized pieces

1 vegetable or chicken stock cube

275ml ($^1/_2$ pint) boiling water

570ml (1 pint) skimmed milk

salt and black pepper

Heat oil in large non-stick pan, and add onions.

Sauté for 5 minutes, stirring occasionally.

Add leeks and cook for 7 minutes, stirring occasionally.

Mix stock cube with water and add to pan with milk and beans.

Season and bring to the boil.

Reduce heat and simmer for 20 minutes.

Cool soup slightly, reserving a few slices of leeks and beans, then purée.

Return to pan with bacon, reserved beans and leeks. Heat through.

25g (1oz) butter

1 small onion, chopped

450g (1lb) courgettes, thinly sliced

400g (14oz) can tomatoes

1 tbsp flour

720ml (1$^1/_2$ pints) ham stock

$^1/_4$ tsp turmeric

salt and pepper

grated Parmesan cheese

Tomato and Courgette Soup

Serves 4

Melt butter in pan and add onion and courgettes.

Cover and cook for 5 minutes.

Add tomatoes, stir in flour and continue cooking for 2–3 minutes.

Stir in remaining ingredients and bring to the boil.

Simmer for 20 minutes then liquidize.

Serve with warm crusty bread.

Thick Lentil Soup

Based on Indian dhal.

Put lentils in deep saucepan. Pour boiling water over them and leave overnight. Drain in colander to clean lentils.

Make up stock in 1 pint of water. Add this, and 2 pints of water, to other ingredients.

Bring to the boil on high heat setting, watching and stirring all the time. Remove any white scum at boiling point.

Turn heat down very low, and simmer for up to 2 hours. (Depending on which type of lentils you use, 1 hour may be sufficient.)

Allow to cool slightly before blending in liquidizer.

Note If this soup is stored overnight in the refrigerator, you may find it thickens too much, in which case dilute by adding a small amount of water.

350g (12oz) lentils (soaked overnight and rinsed as described)

1 vegetable stock cube

1.7 litres (3 pints) water, or more

3 onions, finely chopped

2 medium/large potatoes, finely chopped

salt and pepper to taste

Lettuce Soup

Fry the onion and potatoes in the butter until the onion is transparent.

Add the lettuce and salt and pepper.

Fry for a couple of minutes more then add the milk and chicken stock.

Bring to the boil and simmer for around 20 minutes. Leave to cool and then liquidize.

Add cream before serving and a small piece of parsley to decorate.

75g (3oz) butter

1 large onion, chopped

3 large potatoes, diced

1 lettuce, shredded (not iceberg)

570ml (1 pint) milk

425ml (³/₄ pint) chicken stock

salt and black pepper

cream (optional)

Iain Crawford's Summer Soup

Perfect on a hot summer's evening. Give it a try, even if you think you don't like cold soup. It's delicious!

450g (1lb) seedless green grapes

2 large cucumbers, peeled and chopped

2 large cloves of garlic, crushed

$^1/_4$ tsp salt

$^1/_4$ tsp pepper

425ml ($^3/_4$ pint) plain yoghurt

half a dozen shakes of Tabasco

handful of finely chopped fresh coriander

De-stalk grapes and keep a few back for decoration.

Purée the grapes; then add cucumber to blender.

Add salt, pepper and coriander and whizz.

Pour in yoghurt and Tabasco and whizz.

Chill in the refrigerator.

Decorate with grapes and eat with lots of hot, crusty, garlic bread.

Stilton Soup

Serves 4–6

175g (6oz) mature Stilton cheese, crumbled (exclude rind)

2 large onions, cut in rings

50g (2oz) butter

25g (1oz) plain flour

1.14ml (2 pints) chicken stock

150ml (5fl oz) single cream

2 bay leaves

Fry the onions in the butter until golden.

Add the flour and cook for a further 2 minutes, stirring all the time.

Add the Stilton, stirring until melted, then mix in the warm chicken stock and bay leaves.

Bring to the boil and simmer for 20 minutes.

Finally, stir in the cream and serve.

Mie Kuah

Asian noodle soup.

Serves 2

Put fresh beanshoots into bottom of serving bowls.

Put water into saucepan and add sour soup paste.

Add vegetables and meat, and allow to simmer for about 5 minutes.

Add noodles and, when they are soft, add eggs; the soup is ready when the eggs are hard-poached.

Use a soup ladle to serve soup onto the fresh beanshoots in the serving bowls.

Add keçap asin, keçap manis and chilli sauce to taste.

1 tbsp sour soup paste (Tom Yum paste, containing palm oil, chillies, galangal, lemon grass)

2 cups of water

1 handful of fresh egg noodles or 1 layer of dried egg noodles

4 mushrooms, cut into sections

2 bok choi (Asian green leafy vegetable), chopped

$^1/_2$ carrot, sliced into fine strips

$^1/_2$ red pepper, sliced into fine strips

small cup of sliced ham, turkey or chicken

fresh beanshoots

2 eggs

To taste

keçap asin (standard salty soy sauce)

keçap manis (sweet soy sauce)

chilli sauce

13

Smoked Haddock Scallops

Serves 4

Preheat oven to 200°C/400°F/Gas Mark 6.

Poach haddock in the milk, drain and reserve liquor.

Remove bones and skin from fish and flake into a bowl.

Gently cook the mushrooms in the butter for approximately 3 minutes.

Add flour and cook for 2 minutes, then gradually add reserved fish liquor, stirring all the time until the sauce has thickened.

Add fish to the sauce and season with mustard and pepper.

Divide the mixture between 4 buttered scallop shells or individual dishes.

Sprinkle with cheese and breadcrumbs.

Mash the potatoes with the butter and milk and use to pipe round the edge of each shell or dish.

Dot with butter and place on a baking tray.

Cook in oven for 15–20 minutes.

225g (8oz) smoked haddock

275ml (¹/₂ pint) milk

110g (4oz) mushrooms, sliced

25g (1oz) butter

25g (1oz) flour

¹/₂ tsp English mustard (made)

black pepper, freshly ground

Topping

25g (1oz) Cheddar cheese, grated

10g (¹/₂oz) white breadcrumbs

450g (1lb) potatoes, boiled

25g (1oz) butter

2 tbsp milk

Potted Salmon

Very easy and very tasty.

Serves 2 (quantities can be doubled)

75g (3¹/₂oz) can red salmon (flaked, with skin and large bones removed)

salt and freshly milled black pepper

pinch of mace

50g (2oz) melted butter

2 tsp lemon juice

2 tbsp single cream

Season salmon lightly with salt, black pepper and mace.

Beat fish well with a wooden spoon to give it a smooth consistency.

Add half melted butter, lemon juice and cream, again beating well.

Turn into two small ramekin dishes and level surface.

Top with remaining melted butter and garnish with parsley. Chill.

Serve with fingers of freshly made toast or melba toast.

Salmon Mousse

200g (7oz) can salmon, drained

2 tbsp tomato ketchup

2 tbsp mayonnaise

150ml (¹/₄ pint) evaporated milk

10g (¹/₂ oz) gelatine (1 sachet), dissolved in 4 tbsp water over hot water and cooled

1 tsp lemon juice

salt and pepper

Serves 4

Mix salmon with tomato sauce, mayonnaise, lemon juice and salt and pepper.

Stir in gelatine.

Whip milk until thick and fold in.

Pour into wetted mould loaf tin or 15cm (6") cake tin and leave to set.

Dip mould in hot water before turning out.

Garnish with lemon slices.

Prawn and Pineapple Starter

Serves 2

Drain the pineapple rings.

Blend the other ingredients slowly, starting with the cheese, until smooth. Fold in the prawns.

Now either pile the mixture on top of the pineapple rings or serve with salad with the prawn mixture alongside and the pineapple rings around it.

Dust with paprika.

1 small pkt Philadelphia cheese
2 tbsp double cream, whipped
2 tbsp mayonnaise
1 tbsp pineapple juice
1 can pineapple rings
110g (4oz) prawns
lemon juice
paprika

Prawns in Soured Cream Sauce

Serves 2

Melt butter and fry onion until soft but not coloured.

Add the curry powder and cook for 1–2 minutes.

Add the prawns and sauté for a further 1–2 minutes, then let the mixture cool.

Toss in soured cream, season.

Serve in individual ramekin dishes on a bed of cucumber slices and sprinkle with paprika.

25g (1oz) butter
2 level tsp onions, finely chopped
1 level tsp curry powder
100g (4oz) frozen prawns, thawed
110ml (4 fl oz) soured cream
salt and pepper

To serve

finely sliced cucumber
paprika

Onion and Potato Cakes

110g (4oz) plain flour, sieved

1 tsp baking powder

1/2 tsp each ground turmeric and salt

2 tsp ground coriander

2 medium sized eggs, beaten

150ml (1/4 pint) milk

1/2 tsp whole cumin seeds

2 large red onions, peeled, halved and thinly sliced

175g (6oz) potatoes, peeled and thinly sliced

3–6 tbsp sunflower oil

Raita

299g (7oz) Greek yoghurt

1 tbsp sweet mint jelly

2 tomatoes, deseeded and diced

1 salad onion, finely chopped

1 tbsp fresh coriander, chopped (optional)

salt and freshly ground pepper

Onion and Potato Cakes with Mint Raita

Delicious as a starter or light lunch.

Makes 8

Mix flour, baking powder, spices and salt into a bowl.

Add eggs, milk and cumin seeds to make a batter.

Stir in the potatoes and onions.

Heat 45ml (3 tbsp) of the oil in a large nonstick frying pan, then drop 4 large spoonfuls of the onion mixture into the pan and cook gently for 5 minutes. Turn over the onion cakes and cook for 15 minutes more until the onions and potatoes are tender when pierced with a knife.

Remove from the pan and keep warm while cooking the remaining mixture.

Mix together all the ingredients for the raita in a bowl and season to taste.

Serve with the onion and potato cakes.

Chicken Liver Pâté

Serves 4

Fry onion in a little of the butter.

Add chicken livers and fry until thoroughly cooked.

Add mango chutney, ginger, sherry or brandy and 175g (6oz) of the butter. Stir until all butter is melted.

Liquidize, then pour into dishes. Leave to set.

Note The remainder of the butter can be used as a layer on the top of the pâté to seal it and a bay leaf can be placed on the top for decoration.

225g (8oz) chicken livers, cleaned

225g (8oz) butter

1 onion, finely chopped

1 dsp mango chutney

$^1/_2$ tsp ground ginger

splash of sherry or brandy

salt and pepper to taste

Rough Smoked Mackerel Pâté

Serves 4

Melt half the butter and add to the mackerel.

Add the cream, lemon juice, salt, pepper and cayenne pepper (adjust to taste).

Split the pâté into individual ramekin dishes.

Pour the remaining melted butter over the pâté to seal and then refrigerate.

Serve with oatcakes or crusty French bread.

225g (8oz) smoked mackerel, finely flaked, skinned and boned

60g (2$^1/_2$oz) butter

110 ml (4 fl oz) whipping cream, whipped until stiff

1 tsp lemon juice

cayenne pepper

seasoning

Peach of a Starter

Serves 4

1 can peach halves

1 pack Boursin cheese

Arrange the peach halves on the grill pan of the oven.

Fill each half with a generous amount of Boursin cheese and grill until the cheese is bubbling and beginning to brown.

Serve immediately as a starter with a dry white wine.

225g (8oz) shortcrust pastry

175g (6oz) Stilton cheese

1 onion, chopped

75g (3oz) bacon, chopped

2 eggs and 1 egg yolk, beaten

275ml (¹/₂ pint) double cream

Stilton Cheese Flan

Serves 4

Preheat oven to 180°C/350°F/Gas Mark 4.

Line 4 individual flan rings with pastry.

Place equal amounts of cheese on the base of each flan.

Cook onion and bacon together in frying pan then place on top of cheese.

Finally, mix together eggs and double cream and pour over each flan.

Bake for 35 minutes.

Serve hot or cold as a starter.

Main Courses

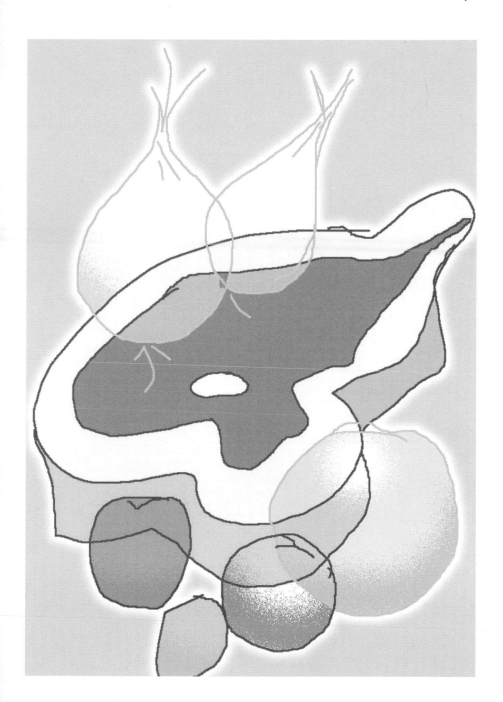

Stuffed Courgettes in Tomato Sauce

(Sheikh Mahshi)

Maryam Mahmood and her family come from Iraq and maintain an Iraqi lifestyle, including delicious family food. A basic everyday meal in Iraq is plain rice served with cooked vegetables in tomato sauce.

6 medium courgettes
225g (¹/₂ lb) minced meat
2 cups water
1 cup olive oil for frying
2 tbsp extra oil
1 small can tomato purée
1 tsp mixed spices

Wash courgettes and remove stalk. Scrape outer skin and scoop out flesh, leaving skin intact and retaining flesh for the sauce.

Heat oil and fry courgette skins until lightly brown. Leave on kitchen paper to cool.

To prepare stuffing, heat extra oil and cook the minced meat. When it is cooked (about 10 minutes) season to taste and add spices. Stuff the courgettes with the meat.

Put the courgette flesh in the bottom of a deep pan and arrange the stuffed courgettes on top.

Mix tomato purée with the water, season with salt to taste and add to courgettes.

Cook on a medium heat for 30–45 minutes until sauce is thick.

Serve with rice.

Albóndigas

Latin American meatballs in a wine sauce.

Serves 2

1 dsp tomato purée

350g (12oz) lean minced beef

1 small onion, chopped

1 egg

1 slice bread made into breadcrumbs

1 small green chilli, very finely chopped

1 tbsp parsley, chopped

50g (2oz) flour seasoned with salt and pepper

sunflower oil for frying

Sauce

1 medium onion, finely chopped

25g (1oz) flour

25g (1oz) butter for frying

275ml (10 fl oz) good strong beef stock

150ml (5 fl oz) red wine

bay leaf

salt and pepper

Mix together the mince, onion, egg, breadcrumbs, tomato purée, chilli and parsley.

Add salt and pepper. If possible, leave the mixture to rest in refrigerator for about 15 minutes at this stage as it makes it a lot easier to handle.

Meanwhile, cook the onion in a little oil until soft, then add the flour and cook for about 3 minutes, stirring continuously. Add the remaining ingredients, whisk until boiling and then simmer uncovered for 10 minutes.

Take the mince mixture from the refrigerator and form into little balls and roll them in the seasoned flour and brown them all over in the hot oil in a frying pan. Once they are browned, add them to the simmering sauce.

Simmer gently for about 40 minutes – until the meatballs are cooked right through. Towards the end of the cooking, remove the lid and bubble the sauce until it has a rich coating consistency.

Beef in Oyster Sauce

Serves 2

Cut beef into thin slices 5cm (2") long and put into a bowl.

Add soy sauce, sherry and 1 tsp dry cornflour.

Let the mixture marinate for 20 minutes.

Heat oil in a wok until very hot and almost smoking, stir fry the beef slices, remove and drain.

Stir fry mushrooms and green pepper.

Wipe out wok, add chicken stock and oyster sauce, bring to the boil then thicken with blended cornflour and simmer for 2 minutes.

Return the beef, mushrooms and green pepper to the wok, coat in sauce and serve with boiled rice.

350g (12oz) lean beef steak (sirloin or fillet)
110g (4oz) mushrooms, sliced
1 green pepper, sliced
2 tsp light soy sauce
2 tsp dry sherry
1 tsp cornflour
1¹/₂ tbsp groundnut oil
60ml (2¹/₂ fl oz) chicken stock
1¹/₂ tbsp oyster sauce
1tsp cornflour, blended in water

Carbonnade de Boeuf

Serves 6

Preheat oven to 160°C/325°F/Gas Mark 3.

Cut meat into fork-sized chunks. Heat oil in pot and brown meat (in batches if necessary). Use slotted spoon to transfer to casserole dish.

Brown onions then return beef to pot, sprinkle on flour and mix well in. Cook for 2 minutes. Remove from heat and gradually stir in beef stock and ale.

Add garlic, juice and half the orange peel. Season well and add nutmeg. Bring to the boil stirring continuously to prevent sticking.

Transfer back to casserole dish and cover tightly. Cook in the oven for 1¹/₂–2 hours.

To serve, sprinkle with parsley and remainder of the grated orange peel.

900g (2lb) stewing steak
2 tbsp oil
1 tbsp plain flour
1 clove garlic, crushed
1 large onion, chopped
275ml (¹/₂ pint) beef stock
275ml (¹/₂ pint) brown ale
pinch grated nutmeg
grated peel and juice of 1 orange
salt and pepper
fresh parsley, chopped

4 tbsp oil

110g (4oz) rindless
streaky bacon, diced

225g (8oz) shallots
(leave stalk and root
intact so that they stay
whole during cooking)

750g (1lb 10oz) stewing
steak cut into 1" cubes

4 garlic cloves, peeled
and crushed

25g (1oz) plain flour

300ml (½ pint) strong
red wine

150ml (¼ pint) beef
stock

2 tsp tomato purée

salt and black pepper

1 bouquet garni

175g (6oz) button
mushrooms, quartered

finely chopped fresh
parsley, to garnish

Boeuf Bourguignon

Serves 3–4

Preheat oven to 160°C/325°F/Gas Mark 3.

Fry bacon in olive oil until golden brown. Remove from pan with slotted spoon and set aside.

Add shallots to pan and cook until golden brown. Remove with slotted spoon and set aside.

Add more oil if necessary and heat. Add steak in batches and brown well all over.

Return all steak to the pan, add garlic and flour and cook gently for 4–5 minutes until flour is lightly browned. Return bacon and onions to pan and add red wine, stock and tomato purée.

Bring to the boil, stirring constantly. Add salt, pepper and bouquet garni.

Cover, place in preheated oven and cook for 2–2½ hours or until meat is very tender.

30 minutes before the end of cooking time, add mushrooms. Adjust seasoning if necessary.

To serve, remove bouquet garni and skim any fat from surface.

Sprinkle with parsley and serve with rice.

Fillet of Beef with a Pickled Walnut Jus

Courtesy of the Caledonian Hotel, Edinburgh.

Serves 4

Sweat shallots until translucent. Add wine and port and reduce. Add beef jus, then add 75g (3oz) of the butter. Stir in pickled walnuts whilst still over heat.

Sweat cabbage in remaining butter and 2 tbsp water and cook until *al dente* then add strips of bacon.

Pan fry seasoned beef fillets in a little oil and butter for 10 minutes.

Place cooked cabbage and bacon in a ring on the centre of each dinner plate. Place one beef fillet on top and drizzle walnut sauce on top.

Serve with the new potatoes.

4 × 150g (5oz) beef fillet
275ml ($^1/_2$ pint) beef jus
150g ($^1/_4$ pint) Madeira wine
275ml ($^1/_2$ pint) red port
110g (4oz) pickled walnuts, chopped
225g (8oz) butter
75g (3oz) shallots
1 head of savoy cabbage, sliced
4 rashers bacon
450g (1lb) new potatoes, boiled

Gingered Beef Casserole

Serves 3–4

25g (1oz) flour

2 tsp ground ginger

¹/₄ tsp chilli seasoning

700g (1¹/₂lb) stewing beef, cubed

3 tbsp oil

400g (14oz) can tomatoes

175g (6oz) button mushrooms, sliced

1 tbsp Worcester sauce

1 tbsp dark muscovado sugar

2 tbsp vinegar

2 cloves garlic, crushed

Preheat oven to 160°C/325°F/Gas Mark 3.

Mix flour, ground ginger and chilli seasoning in a polythene bag and coat beef in this mixture.

Heat the oil in a flameproof casserole and brown meat, a few pieces at a time.

Add the remaining ingredients to pan and bring to the boil.

Remove casserole from hob and place in oven, cover, and cook for about 2–2¹/₂ hours.

When cooked, adjust seasoning and serve with buttered noodles and green salad.

Goulash

Serves 6

700/900g (1¹/₂/2 lb) stewing steak, cubed

2 tbsp oil

225g (8oz) onions, sliced

1 tbsp paprika

1 tbsp plain flour

1 dsp tomato purée

425ml (³/₄ pint) beef stock

1 bouquet garni

1 clove garlic (optional)

1 red or green pepper

2 large tomatoes

4 tbsp soured cream

salt and pepper

Cut meat into cubes and brown quickly in oil.

Remove from pan and cook onion for 3–4 minutes. Add paprika and flour and cook for 1 minute. Gradually add stock and tomato purée and stir until boiling then replace meat.

Add bouquet garni, garlic and seasoning. Cover and simmer for 2 hours or until meat is tender.

Blanch, peel and shred pepper. Peel tomatoes, deseed and slice flesh. Add pepper and tomatoes.

Bring slowly to the boil. Reduce heat and stir in cream.

Serve with mashed potatoes or noodles.

Turkish Beef in Red Wine

Serves 4–5

Marinate the steak in the red wine with the shallots, garlic, salt and pepper, herbs and lime juice (overnight if possible).

Remove meat from marinade and fry in oil until brown then add the onion.

Put the steak and onions to one side and add the flour to the remaining oil and juices in the pan. Cook the flour for approximately 2 minutes, then gradually add the beef stock and the marinade. Stir until thickened then add the steak, onions and carrots. Cover and simmer for 2–3 hours.

About 1 hour before the end of cooking time, place the sliced salami around the top of the pan and continue to cook.

Serve with rice and green salad.

1.1kg (2$^{1}/_{2}$ lb) stewing steak, cubed
1 large onion, chopped
2 shallots, chopped
2 carrots, sliced
150ml ($^{1}/_{4}$ pint) red wine
juice of one lime
garlic
1 tsp chopped chives
1 tsp sage
1 tsp chopped parsley
salt and pepper
570ml (1 pint) beef stock (stock cube dissolved in boiling water)
4–5 slices salami
25g (1oz) plain flour
vegetable oil for frying

'Grotty Cotty' Cottage Pie

Serves 4

450g (1lb) minced beef
(or minced-up left-over roast
beef)

approximately 4 good-sized
carrots, roughly chopped
(no need to peel, as long as
they are well scrubbed)

1 large onion, thinly sliced

350g (³/₄ lb) mushrooms,
roughly chopped

1 can chopped tomatoes,
partly drained

seasoning (salt, pepper,
mixed herbs)

HP brown sauce

baked beans (optional)

sweetcorn (optional)

approximately 450g (1lb)
potatoes

grated cheese

Preheat oven to 180°C/350°F/Gas Mark 4.

Thoroughly cook the mince in a saucepan or frying pan with the onions. Once the meat is properly cooked, add the carrots, mushrooms, tomatoes, HP sauce (to taste), baked beans/sweetcorn (optional) and seasoning. Gently simmer until carrots begin to soften. The HP sauce gives it a slightly spicy taste. Do not let the mixture get too sloppy. Drain off some liquid if necessary.

Boil the potatoes until soft then mash together with butter, a splash of milk, pepper, herbs.

Put the cooked meat into an ovenproof dish and spread the mashed potato evenly over the meat and add a generous layer of grated cheese. Place in oven for about 20 minutes.

Serve hot with green beans, peas, broccoli or any other vegetable.

Note Lamb may be used as an alternative to beef to make Shepherd's Pie.

2 × 110g (4oz) fillet steaks

50g (2oz) prawns

150ml (¹/₄ pint) double cream

110g (4oz) button
mushrooms

4 tbsp whisky

salt and black pepper to
taste

Celtic Fillet Steak

Serves 2

Fry the steaks in butter and oil. Remove and place on a warmed plate, then put into a low oven to keep warm but not to cook any further.

Fry the mushrooms in the pan with the steak juices then add the cream.

Add whisky and prawns and simmer for about 2 minutes.

Add salt and freshly ground black pepper.

Pour over the steaks and serve immediately with salad or baked potato and vegetables.

Steak in Sherry Parcels

Serves 4

Preheat oven to 180°C/350°F/Gas Mark 4.

Coat each steak with the dry French onion soup mix.

Place each steak on a piece of foil and moisten each with a tablespoon of sherry.

Divide the mushrooms between each steak and add 25g (1oz) of butter to each.

Wrap up the steaks to form foil parcels and cook for 1¹/₂ hours.

4 rump steaks

225g (8oz) dry French onion soup mix

4 tbsp sherry

12 mushrooms, sliced

110g (4oz) butter

Steak Pizzaiola

Courtesy of Giuliano's Ristorante, Edinburgh.

Serves 2

To make the tomato sauce, fry the garlic in the olive oil until soft, then add the tomatoes and mix well.

Fry the garlic in the olive oil and wine, then add the steaks. Fry until cooked to taste then add tomato sauce, parsley and oregano. Cook for a further few minutes.

Serve with boiled potatoes and blanched french beans.

2 × 225g (8oz) sirloin steaks

2 cloves garlic, chopped

1 tbsp olive oil

dash of white wine

pinch of parsley

pinch of oregano

Tomato Sauce

1 small can chopped tomatoes

2 cloves garlic, chopped

1 tbsp olive oil

Lamb

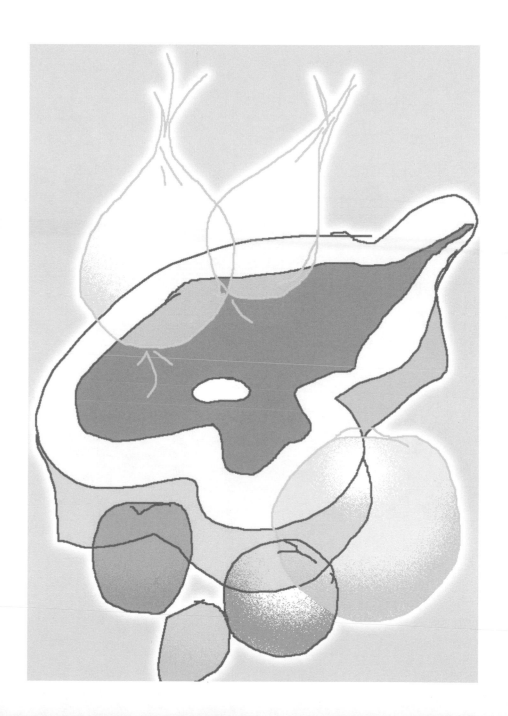

Spicy Lamb with Apricots

Serves 4

Brown lamb in a frying pan, then add the onions.

Mix the spices, flour and seasoning and sprinkle this over the lamb and onions.

Pour mixture into a casserole dish and cover it with the apricots together with the water in which they were soaked. Cook with the lid on at 180°C/350°F/Gas Mark 4 for 1½ hours.

Serve with seasonal vegetables and rice.

700g (1½lb) shoulder lamb, cut into small pieces

225g (8oz) onions, sliced

150g (5oz) dried apricots, soaked overnight

2 tsp ground coriander

2 tsp ground cumin

2 tsp cinnamon

salt and pepper

flour

Lamb and Chickpea Curry

Cube meat and fry. Remove from the pan with a slotted spoon.

Fry onions until translucent, add crushed garlic and sliced mushrooms, stir in curry powder and fry for a minute then return meat to pan.

Add chickpeas and mango chutney and gradually add yoghurt. Simmer for 1 hour.

---

1 large onion, chopped

2 lamb fillets, approx 225g (8oz)

1 tin chickpeas, drained and rinsed

1 tbsp mango chutney

1 level tbsp curry powder

squeeze of lemon juice

salt and pepper

2 tbsp oil

1 clove of garlic, crushed

2 small cartons of natural yoghurt

Wild Irish Stew

Serves 4–6

900g (2 lb) lamb chops

450g (1 lb) potatoes

2 onions, chopped

2 slices of black pudding

1 lamb stock cube in
425ml ($^3/_4$ pint) water

150ml (5 fl oz) Guinness

salt and pepper to taste

chopped parsley

Put the chops, dissolved stock cube, chopped onion, Guinness, salt and pepper in a pot and simmer gently for 1$^1/_2$ hours.

Add the potatoes and simmer for a further 20 minutes. Add the black pudding and simmer for a further 10 minutes.

Garnish with chopped parsley and serve with buttered carrots.

1 large gigot chop per person

1 large onion, chopped

1 medium tomato, chopped

2 cloves garlic, chopped

110g (4oz) mushrooms, chopped

sea salt

pinch mixed dried herbs

ground black pepper

$^1/_2$ tsp ground coriander

1 bay leaf

1 small glass red wine

30ml (2 tbsp) wholemeal flour

50g (2oz) butter

15ml (1 tbsp) olive oil

prunes, canned (optional)

Gigot Chops de Luxe

In a large heavy frying pan, place 25g (1oz) butter and half of the oil. Heat to bubbling and add onion, garlic, tomato, mushrooms, salt, pepper and herbs. Cook for 5 minutes and transfer to casserole dish.

Dust the chops with flour and brown in remaining oil and butter, then transfer to casserole. Use a little boiling water and wine to clean pan and add to casserole with coriander and bay leaf.

Cook at 180°C/350°F/Gas Mark 4 for about 1$^1/_2$ hours.

Serve with new potatoes, mangetout and cauliflower.

Remember to remove bay leaf – I have still to see anyone able to chew it! My mother used to add prunes to this dish 30 minutes before the end of cooking, optional but delicious.

Navarin d'Agneau Printanier

(Navarin of Lamb with Spring Vegetables)

Courtesy of L'Auberge Restaurant, Edinburgh.

Serves 8

Sauté the lamb in a frying pan in oil. When brown, remove and sauté carrots, onions and garlic.

Return the lamb to pan and stir in tomato paste.

When it begins to colour, mix in the flour and put in casserole dish and into oven for a few minutes at 200°C/400°F/Gas Mark 6.

Remove from oven and add wine and stock. Add bouquet garni and salt and pepper. Return to oven till it begins to bubble.

Turn down heat to 170°C/325°F/Gas Mark 3 and cook gently for 2–2½ hours.

Steam the vegetables and then sauté them to serve with the lamb.

1½ kg (3¼lb) diced shoulder lamb

sunflower oil

50g (2oz) plain flour

50g (2oz) tomato paste

3 medium sized onions, diced

3 carrots, diced

4 cloves garlic, crushed

1 bouquet garni

½ bottle red wine and same amount of lamb stock

salt and pepper

Vegetable garnish

700g (1½ lb) new potatoes

225g (½ lb) baby onions

450g (1 lb) baby carrots

450g (1 lb) baby turnips

110g (4oz) green beans

Lamb Casserole

No amounts are specified as they should be adjusted to suit the number to be served and the ratios are not crucial.

lamb steaks

chopped onions

medium size potatoes

carrots, sliced into rounds

stock

cider or wine

chives

mixed herbs

sunflower oil

salt and pepper

Fry lamb in oil until the outside browns.

Remove meat and sauté the onions and carrots in the oil until they soften.

Transfer to a heavy casserole dish, cover with stock and a little cider/wine and add seasoning to taste. Cook in oven with lid on at 180°C/350°F/Gas Mark 4 for 1 hour.

Parboil potatoes, drain, slice and layer on top of the casserole. Top up the liquid in the casserole with the cooking water from the potatoes. Cook with the lid off for a further 1–1¹/₂ hours.

275g (10oz) lean fillet of lamb

1 tbsp pesto sauce

225g (8oz) jar Napoletana tomato sauce

1 onion, finely chopped

2 cloves garlic, crushed

2 cups long grain rice, steamed

spinach leaves, cooked in garlic, balsamic vinegar and olive oil

Lamb Genovese

Courtesy of Giuliano's Ristorante, Edinburgh. This dish is presented like the Italian flag (vertical red, white and green stripes) and is ready within minutes.

Serves 2

Dice the lamb. Sweat the garlic and onion in the oil for 2 minutes.

Add the lamb, pesto, wine and tomato sauce.

Cook for a further 2–3 minutes.

Serve with the blanched spinach leaves.

Elizabethan Spring Lamb

Preheat oven to 200°C/400°F/Gas Mark 6.

Mix rosemary, garlic, a little salt and pepper into the butter.

When mixed well, spread liberally over the white fat of the lamb.

Place meat in a roasting tin and cook for 20 minutes per 450g (1lb) lamb plus 20 minutes over.

When cooked, remove joint and place on a serving dish. Save the surrounding meat juices and transfer to a saucepan.

Add the sherry, stock and jam to the meat juices, bring to the boil and simmer to reduce the alcohol for a few minutes.

Remove from the heat and stir in the 25g (1oz) butter to thicken.

Add a little more salt and pepper to taste.

Serve the sauce as an accompaniment to the meat. Serve with new potatoes in their skins and spring greens.

1 medium-sized leg of English lamb

75g (3oz) butter

1 clove of garlic, crushed

1 dsp fresh rosemary, chopped

salt and pepper

Sauce

1/2 cup sweet cooking sherry

1 tbsp strawberry jam

150ml (1/4 pint) brown stock

25g (1oz) butter

Rogan Josh

450g (1 lb) lamb cut into 5cm (2") cubes

175g (6oz) onions, peeled and finely chopped

3 tbsp vegetable oil

4 cardamom pods

2 bay leaves

6 whole black peppercorns

4 whole cloves

2.5cm (1") cinnamon bark

4 cloves garlic, peeled and finely chopped

1" cube ginger, peeled and finely chopped

2 green chillies

1 tsp coriander powder

1 tsp cumin powder

1 tsp salt

$^1/_2$ tsp garam masala

1 tbsp paprika

1 tbsp tomato purée

2 tbsp plain yoghurt

425ml (14 fl oz) cold water

Heat the oil in a large saucepan and add cardamom, bay leaves, black peppers, cloves and cinnamon. Wait until the cloves swell up or bay leaves begin to take on colour. This just takes a few seconds.

Now add chopped onion, stir and fry until they are browned. Turn heat to low and add garlic, ginger, chillies, coriander, cumin, salt, garam masala, paprika and tomato purée. Stir to mix.

Add 1 tbsp yoghurt and cook for about 30 seconds until well blended. Add remaining yoghurt, and keep stirring for a minute.

Add lamb and cook for 5 minutes.

Add water, bring to the boil, cover and cook over low heat for about 40 minutes until meat is tender and sauce has reduced.

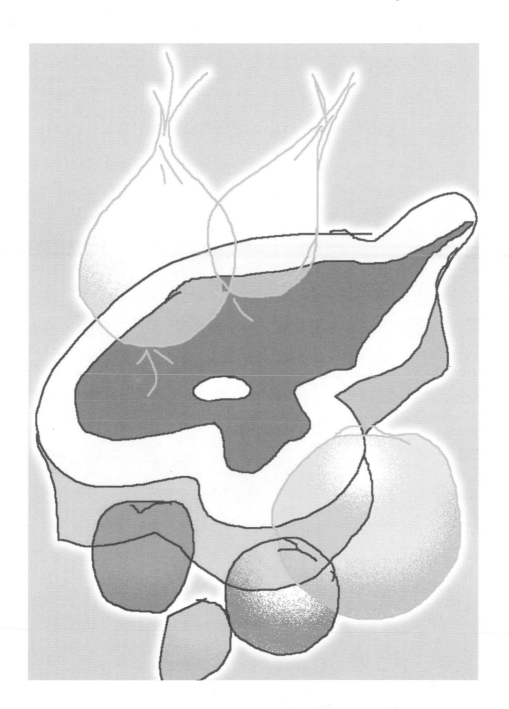

Fillet de Porc Tourangeau

Serves 4

Place the prunes in a shallow bowl, cover with wine and soak overnight. Drain the prunes, reserving the liquid and remove stones.

Melt butter in casserole dish, add pork and cook over brisk heat until lightly coloured on all sides.

Sprinkle with salt and pepper. Add prunes.

Pour over reserved liquid and bring to the boil. Lower heat, cover and simmer gently for 30 minutes.

Remove pork and prunes and place on warm serving platter. Keep hot at lowest possible setting on oven.

Add redcurrant jelly and lemon juice to the pan and stir until jelly melts. Stir in cream and bring to the boil for 5 minutes until thickened and turning golden, whisking continuously. Season and pour over pork. Serve immediately.

16 prunes
275ml (¹/₂ pint) dry white wine
50g (2oz) butter
700g (1¹/₂lb) pork fillet, cut into bite-sized pieces
salt and pepper
2 tbsp redcurrant jelly
1 tbsp lemon juice
150ml (¹/₄ pint) double cream

Pork Goulash

Serves 4

Fry onion, garlic purée and caraway seeds in olive oil until the onion is soft. Take out of the pan and reserve.

Put pork fillet in pan and brown all over.

Return the onion mixture to the pan, add the paprika, tomato purée, tomatoes, stock and salt and pepper.

Simmer for 20 minutes or until pork is soft.

Add the parsley and spoon the sour cream on top just before serving.

900g (2lb) pork fillet, cubed
450g (1lb) onions, sliced
garlic purée to taste
1¹/₂ tbsp caraway seeds
2 tbsp paprika
2 tbsp tomato purée
1 can tomatoes, chopped
275ml (¹/₂ pint) pork stock
2 tbsp parsley, chopped
1 small carton sour cream
black pepper and garlic salt to taste

Normandy Pork with Cream and Apples

Serves 4

4 pork chops

50g (2oz) butter

2 medium cooking apples, peeled and cored

1 large onion, chopped

2 cloves garlic, crushed

$\frac{1}{2}$ tsp dried thyme

3 tbsp double cream

1 tsp sugar

salt and black pepper

425ml ($\frac{3}{4}$ pint) cider

Preheat oven to 190°C/375°F/Gas Mark 5.

Melt half the butter in a thick frying pan and fry the pork chops on both sides until golden brown. Using a draining spoon, transfer to a casserole and sprinkle with a scant $\frac{1}{2}$ teaspoonful of thyme.

Add the onion and garlic to the pan and fry for about 5 minutes until softened. Transfer to the casserole. Cut cooking apples into rings and place on top. Sprinkle with sugar.

Spoon off any fat left in the pan and then pour in the cider. Bring to simmering point then transfer to the casserole. Add salt and pepper. Put a lid on the casserole and cook for about 40 minutes or until the chops are tender.

When ready to serve, take the casserole out of the oven and let it rest for a couple of minutes, then stir in the cream and serve immediately.

Chinese Pork Chops

Serves 2

4 large pork chops

2 tbsp tamari or soy sauce

1 tbsp thin honey

1–2 cloves garlic

Blend the sauce, honey and crushed garlic in a shallow dish.

Add the chops, pouring the mixture over them, and marinate them for a couple of hours (or overnight if convenient).

Cook the chops in the marinade in a covered casserole at 180°C/360°F/Gas Mark 4–5 for 1 hour.

The cover can be removed for the last 10 minutes to brown the chops, but check from time to time that there is enough liquid.

Pork Chops Ardennoise

Serves 4–5

Remove rind from the gammon rashers and cut them into small squares or strips.

Place in a bowl and cover with the wine and shallots and leave to soak for about 30 minutes.

Drain gammon and shallots and reserve them separately from the wine.

Lightly season the pork chops and roll in the flour.

Heat the butter over a moderate heat and gently fry the chops for 6–7 minutes on each side.

Add the shallots and gammon and continue cooking for 2–3 minutes. Pour on the reserved wine and the cream. Simmer gently for 10–12 minutes.

Arrange chops on a hot serving dish.

Reduce the sauce a little in the pan, add the French mustard and parsley.

Taste for seasoning then spoon over the chops.

4–5 lean pork chops
2 thick gammon rashers (about 225g (8oz) in all)
2 wineglasses white wine
3 shallots, finely chopped
salt and pepper
2 tbsp plain flour
50g (2oz) butter
150ml ($^1/_4$ pint) double cream
1 tsp French mustard
1 tbsp parsley, chopped

Pork Chops in Ginger Ale

Serves 4–5

Preheat oven to 180°C/350°F/Gas Mark 4.

Sauté onions in frying pan with half the butter. Remove and place in casserole. Brown pork chops and place on top. Sprinkle brown sugar over chops.

Mix tomato purée with flour in a bowl. Gradually add ginger ale. Pour over chops and season. Cook in oven for 1 hour.

4–5 large pork chops
2 large onions, sliced
50g (2oz) butter
a little brown sugar
1 tbsp tomato purée
1 tbsp of flour
275ml ($^1/_2$ pint) ginger ale
salt and pepper

Satay Sticks

Serves 1–2

Thread meat onto skewers or sticks, and grill.

Fry onion in a little oil until soft. Add peanut butter, chilli powder, soy sauce, sweetener and water.

Stir until all the peanut butter has melted and the sauce is relatively smooth.

Serve chicken or pork sticks with sauce and boiled rice.

chicken breast or pork fillet, cut into cubes

Sauce

2 tbsp peanut butter

150ml (¹/₄ pint) water

¹/₂ tsp granulated sweetener

1 tbsp soy sauce

1 onion, finely chopped

1 tsp chilli powder

350g (12oz) pork fillet, cubed

2 tbsp oil

1 onion

1 red pepper

1 carrot, thinly sliced

225ml (8 fl oz) stock (vegetable or chicken)

50g (2oz) mangetout

2 tomatoes, quartered

2 pineapple rings, cut into chunks

2 tbsp soy sauce

2 tbsp unsweetened pineapple juice

1 tbsp vinegar

2 tsp brown sugar

1 tbsp cornflour

275g (10oz) cooked rice

Sweet and Sour Pork

Serves 4

Cook pork in the oil until browned. Add onion, carrot and pepper. Cook for 5 minutes.

Add stock and simmer for 20 minutes.

Add mangetout, tomatoes and pineapple.

Mix cornflour with soy sauce, pineapple juice, vinegar and brown sugar. Combine all ingredients in a pot and boil to thicken.

Serve with rice.

Pork Satay

Serves 4

Place meat in bowl with other ingredients and mix well. Leave to marinate for at least 3 hours.

Thread onto skewers and grill for 10 minutes.

Brown garlic and onion in oil.

Add the rest of the sauce ingredients and bring to the boil on a low heat.

Stir occasionally and add more water if necessary.

Serve meat with sauce and boiled rice.

450g (1 lb) pork fillet (or chicken breast), cut into 2.5cm (1") cubes

1 tsp white vinegar

$^1/_2$ tsp ground cumin

3 tsp coriander

1 tbsp cornflour

1 tbsp oil

1 clove garlic, crushed

$^1/_2$ tsp curry powder

$^1/_2$ tsp salt

$^1/_2$ tsp sugar

2 tbsp soy sauce

Sauce

1 tbsp oil

1 clove garlic, crushed

1 onion, finely chopped

$^1/_2$ green pepper, finely chopped

2 tbsp white vinegar

1 tsp chilli sauce

$^1/_4$ tsp salt and pepper

1 tsp curry powder

3 tbsp peanut butter

4 tbsp water

Gammon, Veal, Sausage

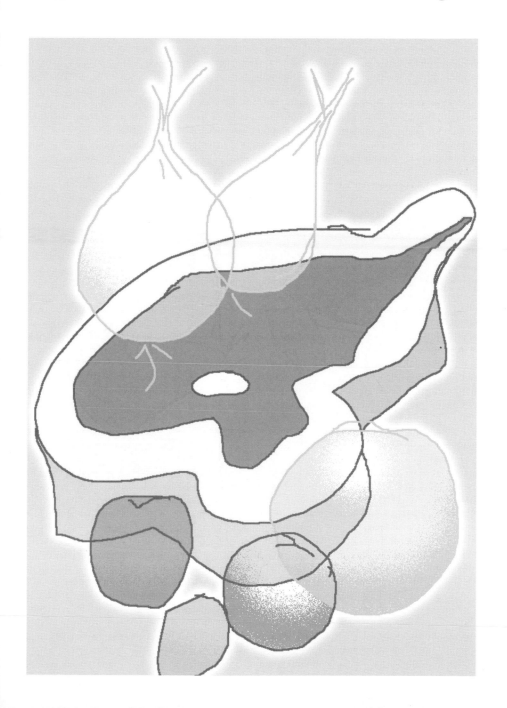

Brisbane Fruity Gammon

Serves 6–8

Cover the gammon with cold water and bring to the boil. Drain, cover with fresh water and bring to the boil again. Lower heat and cover. Simmer slowly allowing 20 minutes per 450g (1lb) and 20 minutes over. Drain and leave to stand for 10 minutes.

Carefully peel off the rind. Score fat into a diamond pattern and spread with the breadcrumbs mixed with the mustard, sugar and butter.

Transfer to a roasting tin and surround with the fruit (including the syrup from the can).

Cook in the centre of oven at 220°C/425°F/Gas Mark 7 for 20 minutes, basting frequently.

Serve hot with vegetables.

1kg 350g (3lb) piece of gammon

25g (1oz) fresh breadcrumbs

1 level tsp dry mustard

1 level dsp demerara sugar

25g (1oz) melted butter

1 can approximately 450g (1lb) quartered pears and peaches (stuck with cloves if preferred)

Wiener Schnitzel

Beat eggs and add melted butter.

Roll veal in seasoned flour, then dip in egg then breadcrumbs.

Fry in oil until well browned on both sides.

Serve with slices of lemon for garnish.

450g (1lb) veal, cut into thin slices

1 tbsp butter

110g (4oz) oil

salt and pepper

2 eggs

flour

1 lemon, sliced

breadcrumbs

Louisiana Jambalaya

From Neissy Graf, Baton Rouge, Louisiana.

Serves 6

900g (2 lb) fresh sausage (one 'hot', one 'mild') cut into chunks

a little leftover cooked chicken or ham (optional)

a little smoked sausage, such as andouille, sliced (optional)

1 large onion, finely chopped

1 large stalk celery, finely chopped

1 bunch green (spring) onions, finely chopped

several cloves garlic (to taste)

$^1/_4$ green bell pepper, finely chopped

1 medium-sized can peeled whole tomatoes

$^1/_2$ tsp (or more, according to your taste) of the following spices – ground cloves, ground allspice, ground thyme (or thyme leaves)

dash of Tabasco (but go easy if your sausage is very pepper-hot)

$1^1/_2$ tsp salt

$^1/_2$ tsp ground black pepper

1 large bay leaf

3 tbsp parsley

2 cups uncooked long-grain white rice

Place sausage in Dutch oven (i.e. big casserole) over moderately high heat to brown. If the sausage is lean, use cooking oil (about 2–3 tbsp) for browning.

Add slices of andouille if you have it. When brown, remove sausage from dish and set aside.

Place vegetables in dish and brown well over medium heat, putting onion, celery and green onion bulb ends (the white part) in first and adding garlic, bell pepper and green onion tops last.

Use fork or slotted spoon to remove tomatoes from liquid in can. Chop the tomatoes in the food processor, but do not purée. Add tomatoes (not the liquid) to the pot.

When tomatoes and other vegetables are brown, add tomato liquid and a little water (or wine).

Add spices, salt, pepper, bay leaf and parsley and stir well. Let this simmer for half an hour or more, until the flavours are well mixed, adding liquid as needed.

Return the sausage to the pot and add any cooked meat (such as leftover ham or chicken), if desired.

While the sauce is returning to a low boil, rinse the rice several times in water baths to remove some of the starch. Be sure there is sufficient liquid in the pot, then add the rice and stir gently.

With the pot uncovered, reduce heat to simmer and let the mixture cook.

You may stir occasionally, but be very gentle since you don't want to mash the rice.

After about 20 minutes, the rice will have absorbed the liquid and the jambalaya will be ready!

Serve with French bread and a big green salad.

Any leftovers can be frozen and reheated in microwave for another meal.

Poultry and Game

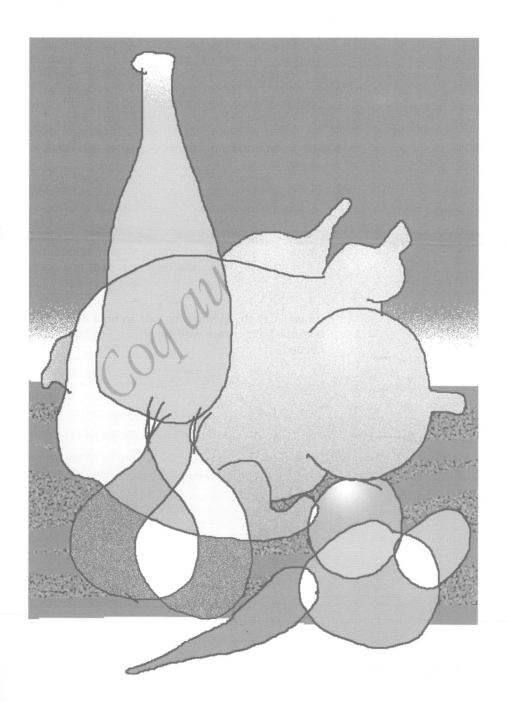

Stuffed Chicken Breasts

Serves 4

Preheat oven to 190°C/375°F/Gas Mark 5.

Cut the chicken breasts into 2 (if large) and flatten out to about ½cm (¼") thick.

Fry bacon in a large frying pan. Add 25g (1oz) of butter and onion and fry gently for 5 minutes until onion is softened. Remove from the heat and add breadcrumbs, egg yolk and parsley.

Add a little salt, black pepper and a shake of Worcester sauce.

Blend ingredients together well and divide into four portions.

Place a portion of stuffing onto each chicken breast, roll up securely and tie each parcel with a piece of string so that there is no stuffing showing.

Place in an ovenproof dish and pour wine over.

Bake in oven for about 35 minutes or more, depending on size of chicken breasts.

Remove the chicken to a warmed dish and keep warm but covered in the oven (reduce temperature to around 150°C/300°F/Gas Mark 2).

Melt the remaining butter in a small saucepan and add the flour, cooking for 30 seconds until well blended. Lower the heat and gradually add the cooking liquid from the chicken, stirring continuously.

Return to the heat and bring to the boil, simmer gently until the sauce thickens.

Stir in the cream and add a little seasoning.

Pour the sauce over the chicken breasts and serve with new potatoes and a selection of crunchy vegetables.

---

2 large (or 4 small) skinless chicken breasts

3 rashers smoked bacon, chopped

1 small onion, finely chopped

50g (2oz) butter

25g (1oz) breadcrumbs (brown/white)

1 egg yolk

25g (1oz) plain flour

425ml (¾ pint) dry white wine

4 tbsp double cream

1 tsp freshly chopped parsley

a 'shake' of Worcester sauce

salt and pepper

Baked Almond Chicken

Serves 2

2 chicken breasts, skinned

2 tbsp ground almonds

275ml (^{1}/$_2$ pint) double cream

110g (4oz) green beans

2–3 rashers of bacon, chopped into small pieces

Preheat oven to 180°C/350°F/Gas Mark 4.

Thoroughly coat the chicken breasts with ground almonds by pressing them onto the meat. Place on a dry non-stick baking tray and bake in the centre of the oven for 30 minutes.

Heat the cream in a pan and season with salt and freshly ground black pepper. Cook the green beans in the usual way. Drain and return to the pan. Fry the bacon in hot oil until crisp. Add the cooked bacon to the beans and stir to distribute evenly.

When the chicken is cooked, transfer to a serving dish and pour the cream around it, not on top. Serve with baked potato, and green beans and bacon.

Bubur Ayam

Indonesian chicken porridge.

Serves 2

1 cup short-grain rice

250g (9oz) chicken breast, cubed

2 cups (^{1}/$_2$ litre) chicken stock (or 1 stock cube and 2 cups water)

fresh coriander

1 tsp ginger, chopped

1 tsp fish sauce

1 tbsp sesame oil

To taste

keçap asin (standard salty soy sauce)

keçap manis (sweet soy sauce)

chilli sauce

2 eggs (optional)

Heat sesame oil, add ginger, rice and chicken stock. Bring to the boil and simmer for 1 hour, stirring occasionally to keep rice from burning.

Add chicken and when cooked (approximately 20 minutes), serve into bowl and garnish with fresh coriander. Add keçap asin, keçap manis and chilli sauce to taste.

Optional Add eggs for a more interesting slant to this dish. About 10 minutes before serving, crack 2 eggs into the chicken porridge and when the eggs are poached, the dish is ready to serve.

Cajun Turkey Burgers

Serves 4

Place all ingredients for burgers (except oil) into mixing bowl and beat thoroughly.

Dampen hands, then form into 4 burgers about 5cm (2") thick. Chill until needed (or you can freeze them for another day).

When ready to cook, brush lightly with oil and grill burgers for 5 minutes. Turn and brush with oil and cook for another 5–8 minutes until cooked through.

Sauté peppers for 5–8 minutes in remaining oil, add onions for a further 3–4 minutes and drain.

To serve, place pepper and onions on bun base, cover with burger and top with relish.

700g (1¹/₂ lb) turkey, minced

1 medium onion, finely chopped or grated

1–2 chillies, deseeded and finely chopped

1–2 jerk seasoning

dash of hot pepper sauce

1tsp soft brown sugar

1 medium egg, beaten

3–4 tbsp sunflower oil

Relish

1–2 chillies, deseeded and finely chopped

1 medium onion, finely chopped

4 firm tomatoes, deseeded and chopped

¹/₂ tbsp tomato purée

1 tbsp dark brown sugar

1 tbsp wine (red or white)

To serve

2 red onions, sliced

1 large red and 1 green pepper, cut into wedges

4 freshly toasted burger buns/baps

Ceylon Chicken Curry

Serves 4

1 chicken, jointed

2 onions, finely sliced

2 cloves garlic, sliced

25g (1oz) ghee or cooking fat

$\frac{1}{2}$ tsp (flat, not heaped) ground cardamoms

$\frac{1}{2}$ tsp ground cinnamon

3 tsp ground coriander

1 tsp ground turmeric

$\frac{1}{2}$ tsp ground ginger

$\frac{1}{2}$ tsp ground cumin

$\frac{1}{2}$ tsp chilli powder (or less)

salt to taste

50g (2oz) creamed coconut

Flake the creamed coconut and dissolve in approximately 160ml (6 fl oz) hot water.

Fry onions, garlic, cardamoms and cinnamon in ghee (or fat). When onions are golden brown, add other dry ingredients. Stir well and cook on low heat for 5 minutes, stirring occasionally to prevent burning. Add chicken and cook for a further 5 minutes until chicken is 'sealed'.

Add the coconut water, cover pan and simmer on low heat until chicken is cooked.

This should be a fairly dry curry. If it is too wet, gently stir in 1–2 tablespoonfuls of fine desiccated coconut 5–10 minutes before end of cooking.

Chicken à la Hun

Serves 2

2 chicken breasts, skinned and boned

1 medium can peeled tomatoes, part-drained

10 mushrooms (any variety), sliced

1 large onion, diced

4 tbsp Worcester sauce

pinch of sugar

seasoning

dash of olive oil

small carton of single cream (optional)

Parmesan cheese to taste (optional)

fresh egg pasta, rice or pitta bread

Heat oil in frying pan or wok. Add onion and stir until translucent.

Slice chicken breast (approximately 1cm or $\frac{1}{2}$" wide) and add to pan, browning on all sides.

Add tomatoes and simmer. Add mushrooms, Worcester sauce, sugar and seasoning.

Simmer for 15–20 minutes, stirring frequently.

Add half small carton of single cream and stir for a further 10 minutes.

Serve on a bed of fresh egg pasta, rice or pitta bread. Garnish with grated cheese.

Chicken in Cider

Serves 8

Fry chicken joints on both sides in melted butter and oil until golden. Remove and drain, then place in one layer in flame-proof cooking pot which should be deep enough for joints to be completely covered in liquid later.

Brown the bacon, onions, followed briefly by the garlic and thyme, then add to chicken. Season with salt and pepper and add bay leaves. Pour in the cider, cover and simmer gently for 45–60 minutes. Stir in mushrooms for the last 15 minutes of the cooking time.

When chicken is tender, remove all ingredients to a warmed serving dish and keep warm. Discard herbs. Bring liquid to a fast boil and reduce by a third. Add the paste, bring to the boil, whisking until the sauce is thickened.

Serve with sauce poured over. Sprinkle with parsley.

8 chicken joints

1 tbsp oil

2 cloves garlic, crushed

2 sprigs fresh thyme

225g (8oz) unsmoked streaky bacon, derinded and cubed

16 button onions or 2–3 large onions, chopped

720ml (1¼ pints) dry cider

1 rounded tsp softened butter or margarine and 1 tbsp flour, mixed to a paste

25g (1oz) butter

2 bay leaves

salt and pepper

Thai Chicken

Thai cooking is increasingly popular and this recipe is really easy and tasty.

Serves 4

Put everything (apart from the chicken breasts!) in the blender and whizz together.

Put chicken breasts in dish and pour over the liquid. Marinate for 1 hour.

Preheat grill, lift out chicken and cook.

Warm the marinade in a pan, stirring gently, but do not boil or it will separate.

Put cooked chicken in serving dish and pour over warm sauce.

Serve with plain boiled rice, and a green salad topped with toasted pine nuts.

4 chicken breasts

200g (7oz) can coconut milk

3 fat cloves of garlic, peeled and chopped

3 fresh green chillies, chopped (don't bother deseeding them, but wash your hands before you do anything else!)

1 level tsp ground ginger

3 tbsp soy sauce

grated zest and juice of 2 limes

big handful of fresh coriander

6 chicken joints (or breasts)

50g (2oz) seasoned plain flour

1–2 beaten eggs plus dried breadcrumbs, or Ruskoline, for coating chicken and bananas

2–3 bananas

oil for frying

watercress or parsley for garnish

bacon rolls (optional)

Corn Fritters

1 small can corn kernels

25g (1oz) plain flour

1 egg

seasoning

$^1/_2$ cup (125ml) milk

Tomato Sauce

275ml ($^1/_2$ pint) canned tomato juice (or 1 small can tomato purée and 1 cup water)

$^1/_4$ medium onion

bacon rinds

1 bayleaf

2 tsp cornflour

seasoning

pinch sugar

Chicken Maryland

Serves 6

Remove skin from chicken and toss in seasoned flour, shaking off excess. Dip each one carefully in beaten egg then in breadcrumbs. Set aside.

Drain sweetcorn and empty into a bowl. Stir in flour and seasoning. Add 1 beaten egg and enough milk to make a thick batter. Beat well. Set aside.

Cut bananas in half lengthwise and once across. Coat in egg and breadcrumbs similar to chicken. Set aside.

Place tomato juice, onion, bacon rinds and bayleaf in small saucepan. Allow to simmer gently for 10–15 minutes. Blend cornflour with a little water. Stir into sauce. Bring to the boil and simmer for 1 minute. Season to taste adding a pinch of sugar if necessary. Strain into a sauceboat and keep warm, ready to serve with the Chicken Maryland.

Heat oil (enough to come half-way up chicken) in large frying pan. Fry chicken pieces carefully turning frequently until golden brown all over. Drain and transfer to baking tray.

Bake in oven at 180°C/350°F/Gas Mark 4 for 20–25 minutes.

Fry fritters by slipping dessertspoonfuls of batter mixture into hot fat. Cook for 2–3 minutes, turn over and fry other side. Drain and place on serving dish. Keep warm.

Fry bananas till golden brown. Drain and place on serving dish. Keep warm.

Serve chicken joints surrounded by fritters and bananas and garnish with watercress and bacon rolls.

Chicken Tikka Masala

Serves 2

Marinate chicken for at least 1 hour, preferably overnight.

Heat oil in frying pan over medium heat. When hot, place chicken in single layer and brown lightly on both sides. Remove and set aside.

Fry onion in remaining oil until lightly brown stirring frequently. Turn heat to low, add chilli, garlic, ginger, paprika, salt, sugar, garam masala, purée and fresh coriander; stir to mix.

Beat cream and yoghurt lightly together until smooth and add to other ingredients.

Add chicken and water, stir to mix. Bring to the boil, turn heat to low and cover. Simmer for about 20 minutes on medium-low heat until the sauce has reduced and turned fairly thick.

275g (10oz) skinless chicken breasts cut into 2.5cm (1") lengths

110g (4oz) onion, peeled and finely chopped

2 tbsp vegetable oil

1 chilli, finely chopped

2 cloves garlic, peeled and finely chopped

$^1/_2$ cm ($^1/_4$") cube ginger

$^1/_4$ tsp paprika

$^1/_2$ tsp salt

$^1/_2$ tsp sugar

$^1/_2$ tsp garam masala

1 tsp tomato purée

2 tbsp plain yoghurt

1 small carton double cream

fresh coriander

150ml (5 fl oz) cold water

Marinade

Mix $^1/_4$ tsp salt, $^1/_4$ tsp chilli powder and 1 tbsp yoghurt in bowl.

10 boned and skinned chicken breasts

Marinade

1 tsp cumin

$^1/_2$ tsp turmeric

5 cloves garlic, crushed

100g (3$^1/_2$oz) sundried tomatoes

salt and pepper

1 tsp harissa

1 pkt coriander leaves, chopped

Couscous

400g (14oz) couscous

1g saffron

$^1/_2$ tsp turmeric

$^1/_2$ tsp cumin

30g (1$^1/_2$oz) sultanas

chicken stock

fresh parsley

Chicken with Couscous

Courtesy of Denis Zominy, Senior Sous Chef, Marriott Dalmahoy, Edinburgh

Serves 10

Slice the chicken breasts into long but flat pieces.

Put in marinade and leave overnight.

Put couscous, saffron, turmeric, sultanas in a pan and pour over boiling chicken stock. Keep hot.

Pan fry chicken pieces in butter and oil and when cooked, remove chicken. Keep warm.

Make a roux with butter and flour. Gradually stir in some of the marinade and chicken stock.

To serve

Put the hot couscous in centre of plate using a ring as a mould.

Put the cooked chicken on top, making sure you achieve some height.

Pour some sauce on the plate.

Garnish on top with some fresh flat parsley.

Creamy Chicken

Serves 4

Combine soup, mayonnaise, double cream and curry powder together in a bowl.

Place chicken and broccoli into casserole dish.

Pour the curry mixture over and mix together.

Sprinkle some cheese on top and cook at 190°C/375°F/Gas Mark 5 for 30 minutes.

2 cooked chicken breasts, chopped
cooked broccoli spears
large can Campbell's chicken or mushroom soup
4 tbsp mayonnaise
4 tbsp double cream
$^{1}/_{2}$–1 tsp curry powder
grated cheese

Chow Mein

Serves 2

Cover onions, celery and peppers in boiling water for 1 minute. Drain and set aside.

Fry onions in butter until transparent, add celery and mushrooms and cook for 2 minutes.

Add cornflour and cook for 1 minute. Gradually add stock and bring to the boil.

Add peppers, chicken, soy sauce and seasoning.

Cover and simmer for 15 minutes.

Cook beansprouts in boiling water for 2 minutes, drain and add to chow mein for last 5 minutes of cooking time.

1 small onion, chopped
2 celery sticks, chopped
25–50g (1–2oz) butter
1 level tbsp soy sauce
freshly ground pepper
425ml ($^{3}/_{4}$ pint) chicken stock
1 small green pepper, chopped
110g (4oz) mushrooms, sliced
25g (1oz) cornflour
1 level tsp salt
225g (8oz) cooked chicken, cut into strips
75g (3oz) beansprouts

10 boneless quail

1250g (2lb 11oz) venison fillet

10 pigeon breasts

20 pork sausages

1 litre (1³/₄ pints) red wine

2 bay leaves

10 juniper berries

¹/₂ tsp mixed spice

4 garlic cloves, crushed

20 slices smoked bacon

Marinade

2 bay leaves

10 juniper berries, crushed

¹/₂ tsp mixed spice

4 cloves garlic, crushed

¹/₂ bottle red wine

Sauce

450g (1lb) peeled shallots, roughly cut

10 juniper berries, finely crushed

3 bay leaves

¹/₂ tsp mixed spice

3 garlic cloves, crushed

¹/₂ pkt thyme

liquid from marinade

450g (1lb) redcurrant jelly

100g (3¹/₂oz) brown sugar

2 litres (3¹/₂ pints) veal jus

salt and pepper

Garnish

450g (1lb) roasted chestnuts

fresh parsley

Game Medley

Courtesy of Denis Zominy, Senior Sous Chef, Marriott Dalmahoy, Edinburgh.

Serves 10

Stuff quail with half the sausagemeat, finely crushed juniper berries and salt and pepper. Wrap each quail in a slice of bacon. Trim venison fillet and cut into 110g (4oz) pieces. Trim pigeon breasts and clean the bone.

Put all 3 items into marinade ingredients. Leave for at least 4 hours or overnight.

Wrap the remainder of the sausages in bacon.

Pan fry the venison, bacon-wrapped quail and sausages and pigeon breasts in oil and butter. Season to taste. Transfer venison and quail to ovenproof dish to finish off in a moderate oven for approximately 10 minutes, then add the pigeon and sausages and cook for a further 5–7 minutes.

Sauce

Sweat the shallots with the garlic, bay leaves, mixed spice, crushed juniper berries and thyme in a pan. Then add redcurrant jelly, sugar and marinade liquid to make a syrup. Add veal jus and simmer for a few minutes. Add salt and pepper to taste. Sauce should be strong and dark. Pass through a sieve.

To serve

Cut quail in half; finely scallop venison and cut pigeon breasts lengthwise. Pour over the sauce and garnish with bacon-wrapped sausages, rosemary, fresh parsley and roasted chestnuts.

Crispy Chicken

Serves 4

Melt butter in pan. Remove from heat and mix in cheese, parsley and crisps.

Divide mixture into four and cover the top of each chicken breast.

Put into a shallow ovenproof dish and cook in the oven at 180°C/350°F/Gas Mark 4 for approximately 45 minutes until chicken is cooked.

Pour off any fat then add mushroom and white wine cook-in sauce, pouring around the sides of the chicken to keep the tops of the chicken crispy.

If you wish, add extra sliced mushrooms at this point.

Pop back into the oven until the sauce is heated through and mushrooms are cooked.

4 chicken breasts

110g (4oz) mushrooms, sliced (optional)

110g (4oz) Cheddar cheese, grated

50g (2oz) fresh parsley, chopped

50g (2oz) butter (or margarine)

1 pkt potato crisps/potato chips, crushed

1 can mushroom and white wine cook-in sauce (alternatively a can of condensed mushroom soup can be used with a little milk added)

Hawaiian Chicken

Serves 6–8

Boil chicken pieces for about 20 minutes. Dry on kitchen paper. Toss chicken pieces in seasoned flour. Brown the chicken in oil.

Drain off excess oil. Add all ingredients except pineapple juice and soy sauce. Brown all ingredients. Add pineapple juice, 1 can of water and soy sauce. Put chicken into a flat casserole. Add cashew nuts and bake at 175°C/350°F/Gas Mark 4 for 30–45 minutes. Serve with rice.

2 chickens, cut into portions (or chicken pieces)

flour with salt and pepper to coat

1 cup parsley, chopped

1 cup green pepper, chopped

450g (1lb) fresh mushrooms

2 tbsp soy sauce

1 cup celery, chopped

1 clove of garlic, crushed

1$^{1}/_{2}$ cans pineapple chunks, drained

cashew nuts

Moroccan Chicken

Serves 3–4

700/900g (1¹/₂–2 lb) chicken breast

4 cloves garlic (or to taste)

¹/₂ tsp turmeric

1 generous tsp cardamom seeds

4 tbsp olive oil

juice of 1 lemon

175g (6oz) small button mushrooms

1 small can chopped plum tomatoes

1 tbsp finely chopped parsley, plus sprigs for garnish

150ml (5 fl oz) Greek yoghurt

salt and pepper to taste

Cut the chicken into 2.5cm (1") cubes. Remove the cardamom seeds from the pods. Peel the garlic and place cloves in a pestle and mortar with the turmeric and cardamom seeds.

Pound the mixture to a smooth paste and blend in the olive oil and lemon juice. Marinate the chicken in the sauce for at least 4 hours or, preferably, overnight. Drain off and reserve the marinade.

Heat a frying pan, add the chicken and cook over a fast heat until brown all over. Add the mushrooms, tomatoes and parsley and pour the marinade over them. Season with salt and pepper. Cook gently for approximately 30 minutes until the chicken is tender. Blend in the yoghurt and heat through without boiling.

Serve at once with couscous or basmati rice, and garnish with sprigs of parsley.

Delicious with mango, peach, or any other sweetish chutney.

roast cooked chicken (1–2 portions per person)

2 red peppers, chopped

200ml (7oz) single cream

2 tbsp wholegrain mustard

200g (7oz) cheese, grated

Mustard Chicken

A hot dish from Finland.

Serves 4

Preheat oven to 200°C/400°F/Gas Mark 6.

Remove bones from chicken and chop meat.

Mix red peppers with chicken pieces and place evenly in shallow ovenproof dish.

Mix cream and mustard together and pour over chicken mixture.

Sprinkle cheese on top and cook in oven for approximately 20 minutes.

Kilkenny Pheasant

Serves 4

Cook the pheasant in a hot oven for 20–30 minutes. Remove the pheasant from the oven and when cool enough to handle, remove all the meat from the carcass and put this into an ovenproof dish.

For the sauce, put the carcass into a heavy saucepan, add onion, carrot, celery and tomato purée. Stir in flour. When the flour has mixed to a smooth paste then add water and wine and simmer for 1 minute. Add cream, salt and freshly ground black pepper. Pour this over the pheasant pieces in the dish and cover. Cook in the oven at 150°C/300°F/Gas Mark 2 for about 1 hour.

Serve with crisps and a variety of vegetables.

1 pheasant
1 large onion, chopped
1 small carrot
1 stick celery
1 dsp tomato purée
1 small cup flour
1 mug water
1 mug red wine
5 tbsp double cream

Lemon Chicken

Serves 2

Put all sauce ingredients (except cornflour) into a pan and bring to the boil.

Simmer for 5 minutes then thicken with cornflour.

Remove skin from chicken breasts and cut each one in half. Pound gently.

Make batter by mixing egg yolks, cornflour, water and seasoning.

Coat the chicken breasts in the batter.

In deep hot oil, fry the chicken breasts until golden brown and cooked through.

Slice each breast across, arrange on serving dish and pour over hot sauce.

Garnish with lemon slices and spring onion tassels.

2 chicken breasts

Batter

2 egg yolks
50g (2oz) cornflour
salt and pepper
water to mix

Lemon Sauce

75ml (3 fl oz) chicken stock
2 spring onions, finely chopped
2 tbsp fresh lemon juice
1 tbsp soft brown sugar
1 tbsp runny honey
1 tbsp vinegar
1 tbsp tomato purée
1 clove garlic, finely chopped
1 small piece ginger, finely chopped
cornflour to thicken

Nasi Goreng

With apologies to all good Thai cooks!

Serves 4

350g (12oz) cold cooked rice

110g (¹/₄ lb) cold ham, diced

110g (¹/₄ lb) salami, diced

110g (¹/₄ lb) cooked chicken

110g (¹/₄ lb) prawns,
if required

1 onion, diced

1 clove of garlic, crushed

cayenne pepper

soy sauce

mixed herbs

Serve with...

shredded lettuce

chopped peeled tomatoes

cucumber cubes

cold omelettes, cooked
thinly then sliced

prawn crackers

Fry the onion and garlic in a wok or large frying pan.

Add enough cayenne to turn them pink. Add meat, rice and herbs.

Cook for 15 minutes, stirring continuously. Add soy sauce according to taste and prawns if required.

Cook for a further 5 minutes.

'One-Pot' Quick Chicken Casserole

A good dish for busy working people as it can be prepared the night before and reheated. It will only take about 10–12 minutes to prepare and 1 hour to cook so you can relax with a drink and read the paper while you're waiting!

Serves 4

Preheat oven to 190°C/375°F/Gas Mark 5.

Heat cooking oil in a large flame and ovenproof casserole dish with lid. Add chicken pieces to low heat. Seal on both sides, taking care not to burn. Remove chicken and drain on kitchen paper. Fry onion until softened. Add garlic then gradually add the rest of the vegetables (add potatoes last) and stir on low heat until softened (add more oil if required).

Return the chicken to the casserole dish, with the vegetables, and add white wine sauce, stirring well until simmering.

Add dry white wine, and a little water if mixture is too thick (the vegetables will absorb a fair amount of liquid). Bring to simmering point, season well with black ground pepper and a generous sprinkling of dry mixed herbs. Put the lid on the casserole and cook in oven for about 1 hour until chicken and vegetables are tender. Check halfway through cooking time and add more liquid (water or wine) if required.

Adjust seasoning and serve with a green vegetable such as broccoli.

4 skinless chicken breasts

1 large onion, roughly chopped

2 cloves garlic, roughly chopped

2 sticks celery, chopped small

1 medium sweet green pepper, chopped small

1 medium sweet red pepper, chopped small

225g (8oz) mushrooms, sliced

2 medium carrots, chopped small

3 medium potatoes, peeled and sliced 1cm (¹/₂") thick and then cut in half

1 can white wine 'cook-in' sauce

150ml (¹/₄ pint) dry white wine

3 tbsp cooking oil

dry mixed herbs

seasoning

Poulet et Pomme à la Crème

Ideal dish for a dinner party as it cooks away gently without you worrying about it overcooking or drying up.

25g (1oz) butter

4 chicken breasts

1 large onion, sliced

1 garlic clove, crushed

175g (6oz) mushrooms, sliced

1 tbsp flour

1 jar apple sauce

1 chicken stock cube dissolved in 275ml (¹/₂ pint) water

¹/₂ glass white wine

1 carton single cream

fresh parsley, chopped

Serves 4

Preheat oven to 150°C/300°F/Gas Mark 2.

Mix apple sauce, stock and wine together. Set aside.

Melt butter in a heavy frying pan. Brown chicken breasts and place in a casserole dish.

Fry onions until golden brown, add garlic and mushrooms.

Stir in flour and gradually add apple sauce, stock and wine mixture. Stir gently until sauce thickens.

Pour sauce over chicken breasts, cover and cook for at least 2 hours.

Just before serving, stir in cream and sprinkle with fresh chopped parsley.

Serve with jacket or sauté potatoes and vegetables.

Pineapple Chicken

4 chicken breasts or pieces

1 onion, chopped

2 tbsp olive oil

1 medium-sized can condensed tomato soup

110g (4oz) mushrooms, sliced

1 small can pineapple rings

1 chicken stock cube

425ml (³/₄ pint) milk

1 tbsp sherry

Serves 4

Fry the chicken together with the onion in the oil for 5 minutes.

Place in a casserole dish.

Add the soup, mushrooms and ³/₄ pineapple chopped.

Add the remaining ingredients except for sherry and simmer for 1 hour.

Just before serving add the sherry.

Garnish with the remaining pineapple.

Spiced Chicken

Serves 4

Preheat oven to 200°C/400°F/Gas Mark 6.

Cut several deep gashes over the chicken.

Rub chicken with salt and lemon juice and leave for 30 minutes.

Remove cardamom seeds from pods and grind in coffee grinder or use mortar and pestle. Mix with other spices and stir into yoghurt.

Smear yoghurt mixture over chicken and leave for at least 4 hours or overnight.

Dot with butter and roast for 1–1½ hours, basting frequently.

1 chicken cut into pieces

juice of 2 lemons

salt

8 cardamom pods

2 tsp ground ginger

2 tsp ground cumin

3 tsp paprika

275ml (½ pint) yoghurt

South African Chicken

Serves 4

Preheat oven to 180°C/350°F/Gas Mark 4.

Brown chicken and remove to casserole.

Fry onions and garlic in oil for few minutes, then add mushrooms.

Mix and add sauce ingredients.

Finally, add pineapple juice mixed with cornflour and simmer until thickened.

Pour over chicken and leave to stand for at least 1 hour.

Bake for approximately 1 hour.

4 chicken breast fillets, rolled in seasoned flour

1 tbsp oil

1 clove garlic

1 onion, chopped

110g (4oz) mushrooms, sliced

1 cup pineapple juice

2 tsp cornflour

Sauce

1 cup boiling water

2 tbsp cider vinegar

1 tbsp soy sauce

2 tbsp tomato ketchup

1 tsp sugar

1 tsp curry paste

juice of ½ lemon

Spicy Chicken and Sweetcorn Chowder

Serves 6

2–3 tbsp canned or frozen sweetcorn

275g (10oz) canned creamed sweetcorn

225g (8oz) chicken breasts, skinned

1 egg, separated

1 tsp cornflour

1 tsp salt

1 tsp sesame oil

1 egg

3 spring onions, finely chopped

1.14 litre (2 pints) chicken stock

1 tbsp curry paste, of desired strength

1 tbsp dry sherry

1 tsp salt

1 tsp sugar

100g (3¹/₂oz) egg noodles, broken up

Thinly slice the chicken into fine shreds about 3" long. Mix chicken shreds with egg white, cornflour and salt and set aside.

Bring small pot of water to the boil. Quickly blanch the chicken shreds, in batches, until they turn white (this should take about 30 seconds). Remove with a slotted spoon and drain in a sieve. Bring stock to the boil in a large pan, add sweetcorn and simmer uncovered for 10 minutes.

Add curry paste, sherry, salt and sugar, bring back to the boil, then add noodles. Simmer for approximately 5 minutes until noodles are cooked.

Add chicken shreds, then slowly pour in sesame egg mixture in a steady stream, stirring with a fork in a 'figure of 8' movement. Leave for 1 minute then serve garnished with spring onions.

Sweet and Sour Chicken

A tasty alternative to takeaway sweet and sour chicken.

Serves 4

4 boneless chicken joints, skinned and chopped into bite-sized pieces

1 can pineapple chunks

1 onion, chopped

1 green pepper, chopped

1 can chopped tomatoes

3 tbsp tomato purée

1 clove garlic, crushed

3 tbsp vinegar

salt and pepper to taste

Put tomatoes in a saucepan and bring to the boil. Add onion and green pepper. Reduce heat to simmer.

Add chicken and all remaining ingredients. Simmer for approximately 30 minutes until chicken is thoroughly cooked. Put into dish and serve with boiled rice.

Fish

Rice-Crusted Salmon Pie

Serves 6

Preheat oven to 180°C/350°F/Gas Mark 4.

To form rice crust, combine together rice, curry powder, melted butter and one lightly beaten egg.

Press mixture firmly into a 9" pie plate, keeping mixture high on rim of plate.

Spread mayonnaise over the tomato slices. Flake the salmon.

Cover base of rice crust with 1 cup of cheese.

Place half the salmon on top and cover with remaining cheese, piling high in centre.

Blend together milk, 2 eggs, salt, pepper and nutmeg. Pour mixture over the salmon and cheese filling. Sprinkle remaining salmon on top of pie.

Bake in oven for 25 minutes then place tomato slices round the inner edge.

Return to oven for further 10 minutes.

2–3 cups cooked rice
2 level tsp curry powder
1½ tbsp melted butter
3 eggs
2 medium tomatoes, cut into thick slices
2 tbsp mayonnaise
1 small can salmon
2 cups strong cheese, finely grated
1 cup scalded milk
salt and pepper
pinch nutmeg

Sauté of Fish

Courtesy of Giuliano's Ristorante, Edinburgh.
A Mediterranean dish for the health-conscious.

Serves 2

Fry garlic in olive oil quickly then add all of the fish and white wine.

Add the lemon juice and parsley.

Sauté all the fish very quickly on a high heat, then simmer for 3–4 minutes (covered).

Garnish with parsley to serve.

16 medium-sized mussels
2 langoustine
10 shrimps
25g (1oz) king prawns
1 haddock, cubed
175g (6oz) halibut, cubed
2 cloves garlic
1 tbsp olive oil
1 cup white wine
juice of ½ lemon
parsley

Baked Trout Fillets

Serves 4

Preheat oven to 180°C/350°F/Gas Mark 4.

25g (1oz) butter

1 carrot, peeled and cut into thin strips

4 spring onions, finely shredded

2 sticks celery, finely sliced

4 medium trout, filleted

salt and pepper

8 sprigs coriander

150ml (¹/₄ pint) white wine

300ml (¹/₂ pint) double cream

Melt butter in a small saucepan. Add vegetables and sauté for 5 minutes. Season.

Put each trout fillet on a sheet of foil. Divide the vegetable filling between the fillets. Add a sprig of coriander and fold fillet over.

Fold up edges of foil and pour wine over each piece of fish before sealing parcels tightly.

Put on a baking tray and bake for 25 minutes.

Open parcels and pour juice into a small saucepan. Bring to the boil and simmer until only 2 tbsp liquid remains. Add double cream and bring back to the boil. Season as required.

450g (1lb) various fish like John Dory, monkfish and salmon,

plus extra prawns for good measure.

1 onion, finely chopped

juice of 1 large orange

juice of 5 limes

4 tbsp best quality olive oil

3 tsp tomato purée

lots of fresh coriander

salt and pepper to taste

Ceviche à la Crawford

You have got to like raw fish – but if in doubt give it a try. It's absolutely wonderful and very slimming.

Skin and cut up the fish into bite-sized pieces.

Whizz everything else together in blender.

Put fish and shellfish (raw and uncooked) in a dish and cover with the liquid.

Leave in refrigerator overnight.

You will see that the fish looks as though it is cooked after about 3 hours.

Eat and relish the amazing taste sensations!

Blackened King Prawn Jambalaya

Courtesy of Denis Zominy, Senior Sous Chef, Marriott Dalmahoy, Edinburgh.

Serves 10

Heat oil in a large pan. Add all ingredients prepared in advance (apart from rice) and cook gently but do not colour.

Add the rice, fish stock and salt to taste. Bring to the boil then simmer gently until most of the moisture has been absorbed by the rice. Reduce the heat and cover for 5 minutes so that **all** of the moisture is absorbed. Meanwhile, heat frying pan to a high temperature. Only when very hot, put the prawns in, one by one. (Remember the pan has to be very hot **all** of the time to blacken the prawns.) Cook the prawns very fast on both sides. (Do not overcook as prawns are very fragile, and will end up chewy.)

Remove stalk from okra which is to be used for garnish – stalk contains the soggy substance. In a separate frying pan, cook okra in some butter and salt and pepper. Do not colour. Keep *al dente* and green.

Remove from pan and lay aside. Put tomato juice in pan with the rest of the marinade and heat to make the sauce.

To serve

Spoon jambalaya into a small round ring approximately 7.5 × 10cm (3" high × 4" diameter), in centre of plate. Gently remove ring to create a smallish, round, mound of rice.

Place prawns around the jambalaya.

Pour sauce all round prawns and add the okra in-between.

Garnish with some fresh, chopped coriander.

Jambalaya

6 large king prawns per person (peeled but leave tail end; cut each one $^3/_4$ of the way down; butterfly them by the tail, then mix with marinade)

450g (1lb) basmati rice

845ml (1$^1/_2$ pints) fish stock

1 pinch cayenne pepper

5g ($^1/_4$ oz) Chinese five spice

4 sliced okra ('lady's fingers' or gumbo)

1 yellow and 1 red pimento, cut into small strips

1 bunch spring onions, sliced

225g (8oz) smoked, cured ham

$^1/_2$ bunch celery, finely sliced

2 cloves garlic, puréed

10g ($^1/_2$ oz) blackened Cajun spice

$^1/_2$ red chilli, finely chopped

6 tbsp olive oil

salt only

Prawn Marinade

1 tbsp harissa

4 tbsp tomato paste

3 tbsp Cajun spice

150ml ($^1/_4$ pint) olive oil

2 garlic cloves, puréed

10g ($^1/_2$ oz) chopped fresh coriander

Garnish

60 okra (6 per person)

fresh coriander, chopped

570ml (1 pint) tomato juice

4 even-sized courgettes

2 small tomatoes

20g (³/₄ oz) butter

1 shallot (or ¹/₂ small onion)

¹/₂ tsp paprika

salt and pepper

110g (¹/₄ lb) shelled prawns **or** white crab meat

For Mornay Sauce

25g (1oz) butter

25g (1oz) plain flour

275ml (¹/₂ pint) milk

40g (1¹/₂ oz) grated Parmesan cheese

10g (¹/₄ oz) grated Parmesan cheese for dusting

Courgettes Maison

Serves 2

Trim each end of the courgettes, then cook whole in boiling salted water for 5 minutes.

Drain and cool under running water.

Remove a thin slice lengthwise from each courgette and scoop out the flesh with a grapefruit spoon and chop it up.

Skin, deseed and roughly chop the tomatoes.

Finely chop the onion and cook in the butter without browning. Add paprika, courgette flesh and tomatoes. Season and cook together for 3 minutes. Stir in the prawns.

Arrange the courgette cases in a buttered gratin dish and fill with prawn mixture. Set aside.

Sauce

Make a roux with the butter and flour and blend in ¹/₂ pint milk off the heat.

Return sauce to heat and bring to the boil, stirring continuously. Simmer for 3–4 minutes.

Season well and stir in 1¹/₂ oz of the Parmesan cheese. Check seasoning.

Spoon the sauce over the filled courgettes and dust with remaining Parmesan.

Put the dish into a hot oven (210°C/425°F/Gas Mark 7) for 12 minutes to brown.

Note Parmesan is a delicious dessert cheese, if you can find it fresh. It is best bought by the piece since the ready-grated cheese loses its flavour quickly.

Crunchy Fish Bake

Serves 4

Preheat oven to 230°C/450°F/Gas Mark 8.

Cut fish into 4 pieces. Sprinkle seasoning over fish. Place in shallow ovenproof dish.

Cream 50g (2oz) butter with egg yolk and add parsley. Spread over each piece of fish.

Sprinkle the breadcrumbs over the top and dot fish with remaining butter.

Pour wine into bottom of dish. Bake for 20 minutes. Add tomatoes and bake for further 5 minutes.

Garnish with parsley and serve with boiled potatoes and peas.

700g (1½ lb) cod fillet, skinned
75g (3oz) butter
1 egg yolk
1 tbsp chopped parsley
75g (3oz) dried wholemeal breadcrumbs
150ml (¼ pint) dry white wine (or cider or fish stock)
4 tomatoes, halved
salt and pepper
parsley sprigs to garnish

Cinnamon Smoked Salmon

Courtesy of the Caledonian Hotel, Edinburgh.

Serves 4

Slice the salmon and lay aside.

Julienne and blanch the leeks and carrot, then add to the chopped chives and shallots.

Mix the olive oil, lemon juice, wine vinegar and whisky together, then add to the mixed vegetables.

On a large plate, place the mixed salad leaves in the centre and surround with the dressing.

Place the two types of sliced smoked salmon over the lettuce and garnish with dill.

Serve with buttered brown bread.

110g (4oz) salmon (marinated in cinnamon, olive oil and thyme for 24 hours)
110g (4oz) smoked salmon sides
75g (3oz) leeks
25g (1oz) lemon juice
110g (4oz) butter
4 slices brown bread
50g (2oz) shallots, peeled and chopped
75ml (3 fl oz) white wine vinegar
150ml (¼ pint) olive oil
25ml (1 measure) Glayva
50g (2oz) chives, chopped
75g (3oz) carrots, peeled
110g (4oz) frisée
50g (2oz) lollo rosso
50g (2oz) oakleaf lettuce

Fillet of Brill with Leeks and Truffle and Herb Broth

Courtesy of Denis Zominy, Senior Sous Chef, Marriott Dalmahoy, Edinburgh.

Serves 10

5 large, skinned brill fillets (or 10 small)

Mousse

450g (1lb) white fish

110g (4oz) shitake mushrooms

2 eggs plus 1 egg white

275ml (¹/₂ pint) double cream

fresh parsley, chopped

salt and pepper

Mousse

Purée the white fish in blender and add the eggs. Pass through a very fine sieve.

Finely chop the shitake mushrooms and add to the fish purée. Slowly beat in the double cream and add the chopped parsley and seasonings.

Herb Broth

white fish bones

leeks, onions, celery, fennel tops, bayleaf, white peppercorns, coriander seeds

parsley stalks

150ml (¹/₄ pint) white wine

Herb Broth

Lightly sweat in a little butter, without colouring, all the ingredients except the bones and white wine.

Add white wine and fish bones and cover with cold water. Simmer for 20–30 minutes.

Pass through a sieve. Place a fillet of brill on a board, smooth side up. Put 1 tablespoonful of mousse into the middle of each fillet.

Into the mousse, push four pieces of blanched baby leeks which have been cut to the same width as the fish. Bring the ends of the fillet around and overlap.

Smooth the ends off and place on a baking tray with the seam on the bottom. Brush with a little butter and cover with paper.

Bake at 200°C/400°F/Gas Mark 6 until tender.

To serve

Sauté about 15 pieces of baby leeks, cut into lozenges. Place leeks in centre of the plate with the brill on top. Pour the herb broth onto the plate.

Garnish all round with fresh chervil, basil and tarragon plus cherry tomato petals. Finish with a little thinly-sliced truffle and a little truffle oil.

Fish Chowder

Serves 4

Melt butter in large pot. Sweat onions and potatoes until golden and soft. Add the cubed bacon, sauté until brown.

Pour in the fish stock and cook the potatoes, onions and bacon until soft and flavoursome but not mushy.

Add the fish and cook but take care not to overcook.

Just before serving, add a good handful of prawns and stir in the milk or cream and freshly milled black pepper; heat until prawns are just cooked (only a couple of minutes).

Decorate with chopped parsley and serve with French bread.

25g (1oz) unsalted butter

110g (4oz) smoked fish, cubed

110g (4oz) firm white fish, cubed

2 onions, chopped

4 potatoes, cubed

several rashers of bacon, cubed

1.14 litre (2 pints) fish stock

freshly milled black pepper

milk or cream

parsley, chopped

handful of prawns

Fish topped with Vegetables

Often cooked on firewood, but can be cooked in a domestic oven.

Put the cleaned and washed fish in a baking dish and season with salt and coriander.

Bake in a moderate oven for 20 minutes or until the fish is half-cooked.

For the topping, fry onion until soft and golden, then add all other ingredients.

Cook for about 10 minutes, then add to dish and bake for a further 20 minutes.

1 medium fish, e.g. trout

1 medium onion, chopped

2 medium tomatoes, chopped

1 tbsp parsley, finely chopped

2 tbsp oil

1 tsp coriander

$^1/_2$ tsp curry powder

salt

1 tbsp lemon juice

1 onion

1 clove of garlic

2.5cm (1") cube of ginger

spices:

   $1/4$ tsp cardamom

   $1/4$ tsp chilli powder

   $1/4$ tsp cumin

   $1/4$ tsp turmeric

   $1/4$ tsp coriander

1 tbsp lemon juice

2 cups rice

350g (12oz) smoked haddock

1 hard-boiled egg

2 tbsp natural yoghurt

parsley/chives

olive/vegetable oil

cube of butter

Kedgeree

Put the smoked haddock in a bowl and pour on 275ml ($1/2$ pint) of boiling water. Let it stand for a couple of minutes (no longer) to soften the fish and start the cooking process, then drain the stock into a jug. Flake the fish with a fork.

Heat the oil. Chop the onion, crush the garlic, grate the ginger and sauté them till the onion is soft.

Add the butter and after it has melted, add the spices and cook them for a few minutes, stirring to mix them in well with the onions. Add the lemon juice. Turn up the heat to let this bubble for a few seconds. Add the rice. Stir it well to coat the grains with the spiced onions.

Add enough stock to the pan to cover the rice. Bring to the boil, reduce heat, put lid on pan and simmer gently for 20 minutes. (Add more stock if kedgeree gets too dry.)

Add the flaked fish and the chopped egg and cook for a further 5–10 minutes until all the liquid is absorbed and the rice is cooked.

Stir in a couple of tablespoonfuls of natural yoghurt and add the chopped parsley or chives.

Serve with a salad.

Fishy Pilaff

Cut the haddock into short 5cm (2") strips and the drained anchovy fillets into 1cm (¹/₂" pieces).

Mix together and crumble in stock cubes.

Put in saucepan, add the lemon juice and 845ml (1¹/₂ pints) water, and bring to the boil.

Drain stock into a bowl.

In a large saucepan, fry the chopped onions in the margarine (or oil) for 3–4 minutes.

Add the rice, turmeric and half of the stock, and simmer for 30 minutes, stirring occasionally.

Add the mushrooms, courgette slices, pepper, watercress and half of the remaining stock.

Cook for 5 minutes.

Stir in fish and cinnamon and rest of stock.

Check to see if the rice is cooked and season as necessary.

Bring back to simmer, then put in warmed serving dish.

Garnish with parsley and include crushed clove of garlic with the onions if desired.

450g (1lb) smoked haddock (broken bits cheaper)

50g (2oz) anchovy fillets in oil (small John West can is recommended)

275g (10oz) long grain, brown rice

225g (¹/₂ lb) mushrooms

2 small courgettes, sliced

1 red pepper

845ml (1¹/₂ pints) fish stock (2 cubes)

1 tsp turmeric

1 tsp ground cinnamon

3 tbsp lemon juice

2 small onions, finely chopped

1 clove garlic (optional)

25g (1oz) watercress (optional)

50g (2oz) margarine

Kirkwall Fish Pie

You will need a large, shallow, pie dish, a large, non-stick frying pan, a sieve, a hot oven and a happy disposition.

2 or 3 large haddock fillets

1 cod fillet

a piece of smoked cod

half a packet of frozen prawns

a piece of red cheese

about 570ml (1 pint) milk

25g (1oz) plain flour

50g (2oz) butter

small pkt of thawed puff pastry

Preheat oven to 200°C/400°F/Gas Mark 6.

Warm the pie dish.

Heat some butter and milk in the frying pan.

Cut the cod and haddock fillets into quarters and lightly poach in the pan.

When just cooked, remove to warmed dish and cover with cloth.

Put frozen prawns and a little more milk in the pan and heat until they are just warmed.

Place prawns in pie dish.

Make a roux by melting the butter then mixing in the flour. Gradually add the liquid from the frying pan (put the liquid through the sieve first to remove any lumpy bits).

Grate the cheese and add to the sauce and when at a creamy consistency, add salt and pepper to taste and spoon over the fish and prawns.

Roll out the pastry and when big enough, place over the dish and pleat edges.

Create sharks and other interesting fishes cut from the pastry remnants for decoration.

Glaze with milk or egg and place in a hot oven.

Remove from the oven when the pastry has risen and is golden brown and serve with freshly cut parsley, boiled new tatties (i.e. potatoes for any Sassenachs!) and fresh garden peas.

Fresh Trout Fish Cakes

Serves 5

Put the trout into a pan of cold water and bring to the boil. After simmering for 5 minutes, drain well then flake into a bowl. (Alternatively, you can use cold cooked trout.)

Cook the onion and garlic in the margarine until soft, then add to the trout with the crackers, courgettes, parsley, lemon rind and juice and Tabasco.

Cook for 2 minutes. Turn into a bowl and leave to cool. Once cool, add beaten egg and season with salt and pepper. Mix well.

Form into 10 even-sized patties, then coat in flour.

Heat the oil in a large, non-stick frying pan and cook the cakes for 4–5 minutes each side.

Drain well on a paper towel.

Serve garnished with lemon wedges and parsley. Serve with creamed potatoes and peas.

---

7 trout fillets

1 onion, finely chopped

1 clove garlic, crushed

15g (½ oz) polyunsaturated margarine

50g (2oz) cream crackers, crushed

250g (8oz) courgettes, end removed and grated

2 tbsp chopped parsley

grated rind of 1 lemon

1 tbsp lemon juice

few drops of Tabasco sauce

1 beaten egg

salt and black pepper

25g (1oz) plain flour

oil for frying

lemon wedges and parsley sprigs for decoration

Moroccan Baked Fish

Serves 4

900g (2lb) filleted, firm, white fish (or whole, cleaned fish can be used)

salt

2 tsp ground cumin

4 tbsp olive oil

3 tbsp coriander leaves, finely chopped

3 garlic cloves, crushed

5 tomatoes, peeled and sliced

1 preserved lemon, washed and sliced

Preheat the oven to 200°C/400°F/Gas Mark 6.

Rub the fish all over with salt, most of the cumin and some of the oil.

Sandwich the fillets together (or stuff the whole fish) with a mixture of the coriander and garlic.

Put the fish in a shallow ovenproof dish and add the tomatoes and preserved lemon.

Drizzle the remaining oil over the fish and sprinkle the rest of the cumin on the tomatoes.

Cover the dish with foil and bake for 30 minutes.

Remove the foil and bake for a further 10–20 minutes until the fish just begins to flake.

Serve with boiled rice, or pitta bread and Greek salad.

Monkfish Medallions

Courtesy of Denis Zominy, Senior Sous Chef,
Marriott Dalmahoy, Edinburgh.

Serves 5 as a main course or 10 as a starter

Marinate all dressing ingredients and leave in the refrigerator overnight.

Next day, put into pan and cook for a few minutes.

Liquidize and allow to cool. Serve cold.

Cut each slice of bacon in half lengthwise, then roll up with basil inside.

Cut 20 medallions of monkfish (2 per person for a starter or 4 each for a main course).

Press a bacon roll into centre of each.

Pan fry in butter and oil. (Do not cook too early or too long or it will be tough.)

Season to taste.

Serve with a salad of finely-cut curly endive mixed with chopped tarragon, basil, chervil and coriander. Then add dressing.

1kg (2lb 2oz) large monkfish fillet

10 slices of smoked bacon

1 pkt basil

1/2 pkt tarragon

1/2 pkt chervil

1/2 pkt coriander

1/2 curly endive lettuce

Gazpacho Dressing

1/2 red pepper, roughly chopped

1/2 green pepper, roughly chopped

1/2 cucumber, deseeded and diced

3 tomatoes, roughly chopped

275ml (1/2 pint) olive oil

275ml (1/2 pint) white wine vinegar

5 garlic cloves, crushed

1/2 red chilli pepper

275ml (1/2 pint) tomato juice

juice from half a lemon

1 glass white wine

Paella

Serves 4

350g (12oz) mussels, cleaned

900ml (1½ pints) chicken stock

4 chicken thighs

1 tbsp oil

1 onion, chopped

2 cloves garlic, crushed

275g (10oz) basmati rice, rinsed

1 tsp saffron strands

1 red pepper, seeded and sliced

½ tsp cayenne pepper

salt and pepper

175g (6oz) cooked, unshelled prawns

100g (4oz) frozen peas

Put mussels and 275ml (½ pint) stock in a saucepan. Bring to the boil and cook for 5 minutes or until shells have opened. Drain, reserving juice. Discard any unopened mussels.

Bone the chicken thighs. Heat oil in a large pan and fry chicken, skin side down until golden. Turn over and cook until meat is sealed. Remove with a slotted spoon and slice meat.

Add onion, garlic, rice and saffron to pan and cook, stirring continuously for 3 minutes.

Add red pepper, remaining stock, fish juices, cayenne pepper and seasoning and bring to boil. Cover and simmer for 10 minutes.

Add prawns, mussels, peas and chicken and cook for a further 5 minutes. Serve.

350g (12oz) cooked prawns (or cooked mussels)

400g (14oz) spaghetti

3 garlic cloves, finely chopped

2 tbsp olive oil

225g (8oz) tomatoes, peeled and chopped (or canned chopped tomatoes)

salt and pepper

small bunch of coriander (or parsley) leaves, finely chopped

1 small, fresh, red chilli, finely chopped (optional)

Pasta Prawns

The sauce takes only a few minutes to cook, so begin preparation of the pasta first.

While the spaghetti is boiling, fry the garlic gently in the oil (add the chilli at this stage if desired) and, as the aroma rises, add the tomatoes, salt and pepper.

Add the coriander and simmer for a few minutes until the tomatoes become soft.

Stir in the prawns and heat through for about a minute.

When the pasta is *al dente*, drain and add it to the sauce.

Stir for a few seconds over a high heat then serve.

Moules Marinière

Serves 4

Scrub mussels under cold running water. Cut off beards and remove any barnacles, if possible. Put mussels in cold water until required.

Put onion in a pan with garlic, parsley, wine, stock, mustard, salt and pepper. Bring to the boil and simmer for 2 minutes.

Drain mussels, add to pan, cover and simmer for 5 minutes or until shells open.

Drain contents of pan, reserving both the mussels and liquid.

Put the liquid in a clean saucepan and stir in butter. Season to taste.

Arrange mussels in serving bowls and pour over the liquid.

Serve immediately.

40–50 mussels in their shells
2 onions, finely chopped
2 garlic cloves, crushed
2 tbsp freshly-chopped parsley
150ml ($^1/_4$ pint) dry white wine
300ml ($^1/_2$ pint) fish stock
$^1/_2$ tsp Dijon mustard
salt and freshly-ground black pepper
40g (1$^1/_2$ oz) butter

Prawn Curry

Thaw and drain prawns.

Melt butter in a large saucepan, add the onion and apple; fry gently for 5–8 minutes.

Add curry powder and paste and cook for 5 minutes.

Stir in flour and cook for 1 minute. Gradually add the stock and bring to the boil, continuing to stir.

Add the chutney, tomato paste, cayenne pepper, salt and a squeeze of lemon.

Cover and simmer for 30 minutes.

Add the prawns and heat through.

Serve on a bed of rice.

350g (12oz) shelled prawns
25g (1oz) butter
2 onions, skinned and chopped
1 cooking apple, peeled and chopped
1 level tbsp curry powder
1 level tsp curry paste
1 tbsp tomato paste
pinch cayenne pepper
lemon juice
salt
1 tbsp plain flour
275ml ($^1/_2$ pint) chicken stock
1 tbsp sweet chutney

Trout Fillets with Walnuts and Stilton

Serves 2

2 trout fillets, dusted with flour

100g (4oz) Stilton cheese

4 tbsp fresh breadcrumbs

4 tbsp chopped walnuts

flour

beaten egg

Crumble Stilton and mix with breadcrumbs and walnuts.

Dust trout fillets in flour then in egg and coat with cheese and walnut mixture.

Cook under preheated grill for 4–5 minutes until crisp and golden.

Serve with a salad garnish and brown bread as a starter or, for a main course, with salad and new potatoes.

Salmon and Vegetable Patties

Serves 4

1 tbsp vegetable oil

1 leek, sliced

1 carrot, grated

1 clove garlic, crushed

525g (1lb 6oz) mashed potatoes

1 × 200g (7oz) can red salmon, drained and flaked

1 tbsp freshly chopped parsley

1 tbsp lemon juice

salt and pepper

1 egg, beaten

100g (4oz) fresh breadcrumbs

Heat oil in a frying pan and sauté leek for 10 minutes until softened.

Stir in carrot and garlic and cook for 2 minutes. Remove from heat and leave to cool.

Mix together potato, salmon, parsley, lemon juice, seasoning and vegetable mixture until well-combined. Chill for 30 minutes.

Preheat the oven to 200°C/400°F/Gas Mark 6. Divide mixture into eight and mould into patties.

Dip each pattie in beaten egg and then in breadcrumbs to coat.

Put onto a baking sheet and bake for 20 minutes until golden.

Vegetarian

Cheese Pudding

Serves 3–4

Preheat oven to 190°C/375°F/Gas Mark 5.

Put breadcrumbs into a basin and pour on boiling milk. Leave to stand for 10 minutes.

Add cheese, butter, egg yolk and seasoning.

Beat the egg white stiffly and fold into the mixture.

Pour into a greased 1 litre (1½ pint) ovenproof dish and bake in centre of oven for 35 minutes until set.

Serve immediately.

50g (2oz) breadcrumbs
250ml (½ pint) milk
75g (3oz) Cheddar cheese, grated
25g (1oz) butter
1 egg, separated
salt and pepper

Hazelnut and Vegetable Crumble

Serves 4

Preheat oven to 190°C/375°F/Gas Mark 5.

Sauté onion lightly.

Cook other vegetables in boiling, salted water, until still crunchy.

Drain and place in buttered casserole dish.

Melt butter over a low heat. Slowly stir in flour to make a roux.

Gradually add milk and stir over low heat until thick. Season and add ground hazelnuts.

Mix in with vegetables.

Rub flour and butter into breadcrumbs.

Sprinkle over vegetable/hazelnut mixture.

Cover with grated cheese (optional).

Bake in centre of oven for approximately 45 minutes.

2 small leeks, sliced
2 medium carrots, sliced
1 medium onion, sliced
1 medium head of broccoli, divided into small florets
110–175g (4–6oz) hazelnuts, ground

Sauce

50g (2oz) butter
10g (½ oz) plain flour
275ml (½ pint) milk

Topping

110g (4oz) wholewheat flour
110g (4oz) butter
50–110g (2–4oz) cheese, grated

½ × 400g packet fresh filo pastry, about 20 sheets (can be used defrosted)

3 tbsp vegetable oil or melted butter

Filling

2 × 250g packets fresh spinach, washed and de-stalked

10g (½ oz) butter

1 medium onion, chopped

1 red pepper, deseeded and chopped

2 tsp ground cumin

570ml (1 pint) vegetable stock made with stock cubes and cooling water from spinach

225g (8oz) split red lentils

110g (4oz) ready-to-eat feta cheese, diced

salt and freshly ground black pepper

Spinach, Lentil and Apricot Filo Pie

This simple but spectacular looking dish is inspired by the spinach, egg and cheese pies made in Greece and Italy at Easter.

Serves 8

Preheat oven to 200°C/400°F/Gas Mark 6.

Place the spinach in a bowl and just cover with boiling water. Put to one side.

Heat the oil and butter in a large pan and cook the onion, pepper and cumin over a gentle heat for about 8 minutes until softened.

Drain the spinach and squeeze out any excess water – reserve this to make 570ml (1 pint) of vegetable stock. Stir the lentils and apricots into the pan with the stock, bring to the boil, stirring, then reduce the heat, cover and simmer for 10 minutes until the liquid is absorbed and the lentils have a 'bite' to them. Leave to cool.

Mix the lentil mixture, spinach and cheese together and season generously.

Brush a 23cm (9") ovenproof spring-release tin with vegetable oil or melted butter and lay 2 sheets of filo in the tin at right angles to each other. Press into the tin and brush with more oil or butter. (Try to keep the corners accessible.) Repeat, setting 12 sheets in all at slightly different angles to line the tin. Spoon the filling into the tin and level the surface. Fold in the pastry at the edges. Crumple the remaining sheets of pastry and set them on top of the filling. Brush with the remaining oil or butter.

Set the pie on a baking sheet and cook in the centre of the oven for 45 minutes. Carefully remove the side of the tin and return to the oven for 15 minutes more. Leave to cool slightly before serving.

The pie or leftovers from the pie can be frozen. Defrost thoroughly and crisp the pastry in a hot oven for a few minutes.

Cheese and Asparagus Pie

Serves 3–4

Line a 20cm (8") tin with the pastry and blind bake for 15–20 minutes or until light brown.

Make a roux with the butter, flour and milk, bring to the boil and stir until the sauce thickens.

Add 110g (4oz) of the cheese and stir until melted.

Remove from heat and add the asparagus.

Pour into the pastry case and sprinkle the remainder of the cheese over the top.

Brown under a hot grill.

110g (4oz) shortcrust pastry

1 can asparagus bits, drained

25g (1oz) butter

25g (1oz) flour

275ml (¹/₂ pint) milk

175g (6oz) cheese, grated

Vegetable Shepherd's Pie

Serves 4

Preheat oven to 180°C/350°F/Gas Mark 4.

Fry onion until beginning to soften. Stir in lentils, tomatoes and stock, and bring gently to the boil.

Stir in herbs and yeast extract and season.

Reduce heat and simmer gently for 20 minutes.

Stir in the courgettes and cook for 10 minutes.

Place mixture in shallow ovenproof dish.

Carefully spread the potatoes over the lentil mixture. Level the top. Sprinkle with cheese.

Bake in the centre of the oven for 30–40 minutes until potato is hot and top is golden and crisp.

Serve with a crunchy salad.

Note Freezes well.

2 tbsp sunflower oil

2 red onions, sliced

110g (4oz) red lentils, washed

2 × 400g (14oz) cans tomatoes, chopped

vegetable stock cube, dissolved in 150ml (¹/₂ pint) hot water

1 tsp mixed herbs

1 tsp yeast extract

salt and pepper

450g (1lb) courgettes, washed and sliced

700g (1¹/₂lb) potatoes, cooked and mashed

75g (3oz) strong Cheddar cheese, grated

Pasta Spinach Bake

Cook macaroni for only 5 minutes, even if instructions say longer as it will continue cooking in the baking tray.

Serves 4

150g (6oz) macaroni

50g (2oz) butter

4 tbsp plain flour

275ml (¹/₂ pint) milk

450g (1lb) frozen spinach, chopped

3 eggs

salt and pepper

45g (2oz) Parmesan cheese, grated

Preheat oven to 190°C/375°F/Gas Mark 5.

Cook pasta in boiling water for 5 minutes, drain and set aside.

Heat butter in pan, add flour and cook for 1 minute, then stir in milk. Bring to the boil, stirring all the time and cook for a couple of minutes. Add the spinach and stir until thawed.

Add seasoning, eggs and half the cheese. Stir together. Add pasta and stir together.

Pour into oiled 23 × 2.5 cm (9″ × 13″) nonstick Swiss-roll tray, spreading the mixture into the corners. Sprinkle over the remaining cheese.

Cook for 20 minutes.

Allow to cool slightly, then slice and serve with salad.

900g (2lb) mixed vegetables (cauliflower, carrot, broccoli, leeks)

225g (¹/₂lb) potatoes, cooked and sliced

1 onion, chopped

50g (2oz) split red lentils

2 tbsp flour

2 tbsp tomato purée

110g (4oz) mozzarella cheese

275ml (¹/₂ pint) milk

¹/₂ tsp mixed herbs

knob of margarine

Tona Vegetable Bake

Serves 4

Preheat oven to 200°C/400°F/Gas Mark 6.

Steam the mixed vegetables until just cooked but still firm and put in an ovenproof dish.

Cook lentils in water until tender and all the water has been absorbed. Put to one side.

Fry the onion in margarine until tender. Add the flour and tomato purée and stir well.

Add the milk, stirring constantly, and, when boiling, add herbs and lentils and mix well.

Pour the lentil sauce over the mixed vegetables and cover with the potatoes and cheese.

Bake for 20 minutes.

Almond Rissoles

Serves 4

Place the almonds and breadcrumbs in a bowl.

Add the onion with the parsley and herbs.

Work in the egg and butter and season to taste.

Mix this to a stiff paste with milk and shape into 8 rissoles.

Coat with egg and breadcrumbs.

Fry in hot oil and butter until crisp and golden, allowing 4–5 minutes each side.

Drain on kitchen paper and serve hot with mixed vegetables or cold with salad.

Alternative Use hazelnuts instead of almonds and brown bread instead of white.

110g (4oz) ground almonds

175g (6oz) fresh white breadcrumbs

1 small onion, finely grated

3 level tbsp parsley, finely chopped

half a level tsp mixed herbs

1 standard egg, beaten

25g (1oz) butter, melted

salt and pepper

cold milk to mix

Coating

1 small egg, beaten

50g (2oz) butter

25g (1oz) breadcrumbs, toasted

2 tbsp olive/corn oil

¹/₂ tsp oregano

1 vegetable stock cube, dissolved in 275ml (¹/₂ pint) water

1 onion, diced

3 cloves garlic, chopped

2 tbsp olive oil

225g (8oz) mushrooms, sliced

1 carrot, finely diced

6 baby sweetcorn, chopped

2 courgettes, sliced

1 red pepper, sliced

1 large can tomatoes

1 tbsp tomato purée

salt and pepper

1 packet cheese sauce mix

275ml (¹/₂ pint) milk

50g (2oz) mozzarella cheese, grated

8 sheets of lasagne

Vegetable Lasagne

Serves 4

Preheat oven to 200°C/400°F/Gas Mark 6.

Fry onion and garlic in olive oil until soft.

Add oregano, mushrooms and tomatoes.

Cook gently for a few minutes then add tomato purée and vegetable stock to the tomato mixture.

Cook gently for 5 minutes then add carrot, courgettes, sweetcorn and pepper.

Season to taste and simmer for 30 minutes.

Make up cheese sauce mix as directed, adding oregano.

Once ready, leave to cool, along with the tomato/vegetable sauce for 15 minutes.

Build up layers of tomato/vegetable sauce, then lasagne sheets, then cheese sauce, and so on.

Finish with layer of tomato/vegetable sauce, the remaining cheese sauce, then the mozzarella cheese.

Bake for 30–35 minutes.

Lasagne al Pesto

Serves 4

Preheat the oven to 180°C/350°F/Gas Mark 4.

Oil a 23cm × 32cm (9" × 13") pan and cover the bottom with sheets of pasta.

Wash and dry the spinach.

For the filling, mix the ricotta, spinach, pesto, garlic, salt and pepper, nuts and half a cup of the Parmesan cheese.

Spoon the filling over the pasta, top with mozzarella and another layer of pasta.

Create further layers with the filling, cheese and pasta, finishing with a layer of pasta and the remaining Parmesan.

Bake uncovered for 50 minutes (cover with foil if top begins to burn).

16 sheets of green lasagne

450g (1lb) fresh spinach (or 540g (20oz) defrosted)

4 cups ricotta cheese

1 cup pesto

4 cloves garlic, minced

$^1/_2$ tsp salt

black pepper to taste

$^3/_4$ cup Parmesan cheese, grated

$^1/_3$ cup toasted pine nuts

450g (1lb) mozzarella cheese, grated

Two-Bean Cheese Pot

Serves 4

Fry onion, add flour and cook for 30 seconds.

Add beans, tomatoes, chutney and seasonings.

Simmer, covered, for 10 minutes.

Spoon into shallow dish.

Arrange overlapping cheese slices on top.

Place under hot grill until cheese melts.

110g (4oz) onion, chopped

25–50g (1–2oz) margarine or oil

50g (2oz) flour

1 large can red beans, drained

1 large can butter beans, drained

1 large can tomatoes

$^1/_2$ tsp oregano

salt and pepper

2 level tbsp mango chutney or pickle

110g (4oz) Cheddar cheese

Cheese and Nut Loaf

Serves 4

200g (8oz) walnuts, finely ground

75g (3oz) Scottish Cheddar cheese, finely grated

1 medium onion, finely grated

150g (6oz) fresh brown breadcrumbs

2 level tsp salt

2 level tbsp parsley, finely chopped

5 tbsp hot milk

1 level tsp mustard

1 level tbsp tomato paste

pepper to taste

12g (¹/₂oz) butter

Preheat oven to 180°C/350°F/Gas Mark 4.

Line baking tray with foil and butter lightly.

Put walnuts in bowl with the cheese and onion.

Add all remaining ingredients except butter and mix thoroughly.

Shape into a loaf approximately 7¹/₂cm (3") high and stand it on prepared tray.

Dot with flakes of butter and bake in centre of oven for 45 minutes.

Cut into slices and serve with mustard or tomato sauce.

1¹/₄ cups (10 fl oz) milk

1 cup (8oz) soft breadcrumbs

25g (1oz) cheese, grated

50g (2oz) butter

salt, pepper, cayenne pepper, chives

2 eggs, separated

Cheese Fondant

Serves 4

Preheat oven to 190°C/375°F/Gas Mark 5.

Boil milk and pour over breadcrumbs.

Add cheese, butter, seasoning, chives and egg yolks.

Beat egg whites and fold into mixture.

Bake for 30 minutes in individual ramekins or pie dish.

Mushroom Casserole

Serves 4

Preheat oven to 180°C/350°F/Gas 4.

Heat oil and fry onion until soft, but not coloured.

Add mushrooms and cook over a **low** heat for 10–15 minutes.

Sprinkle in the flour, stirring gently. Cook until flour has thickened the juices.

Combine the milk and soured cream and add to mushrooms, stirring continuously.

Add salt, pepper, parsley and nutmeg and cook for about 5 minutes.

Pour the mixture into a shallow ovenproof dish.

Sprinkle with cheese and dot with butter.

Bake for 20 minutes until top is brown.

450g (1lb) large mushrooms, wiped and thinly sliced (including stems)
3 tbsp oil
225g (8oz) onion, finely chopped
3 dsp plain flour
1 cup milk
275ml (¹/₂ pint) soured cream or yoghurt
salt and pepper
1 tbsp parsley, finely chopped
a little nutmeg, grated
175g (6oz) cheese, grated
25g (1oz) butter

Dhal

Serves 4

Fry onion, garlic and tomatoes in a little ghee or cooking fat until onions are golden brown.

Add turmeric and chilli powder and mix well.

Add lentils to the mixture with the water. Stir well. Cover and cook on low heat until lentils are soft. (The consistency should not be too thin but like a thick sauce.)

If preferred, the cooled cooked mixture can be put through a blender to make it smoother and then reheated. Serve with curry and rice.

225g (8oz) red lentils, well washed and drained
2 medium onions, finely chopped
1 clove garlic, crushed
3 tomatoes, chopped
25g (1oz) ghee or cooking fat
¹/₂ tsp turmeric
¹/₂ tsp chilli powder (or less according to taste)
720ml (1¹/₄ pints) water

Authentic Vegetable Pakora

Makes 20–25 pakoras

2 medium onions, finely diced

2 medium potatoes, finely diced

1 level tsp bicarbonate of soda

1 heaped tsp chilli powder (or 3 crushed chillis)

3 heaped tsp fenugreek

3 heaped tsp rubbed mint

3 heaped tsp oregano

2 heaped tsp garam masala

260g (9¹/₂oz) gram flour

275ml (¹/₂ pint) water

Chilli Sauce

3 whole chillis, crushed (or 2 tsp of chilli powder)

1 tsp fenugreek leaves

1 tsp rubbed mint

1 tsp oregano

1 tsp garam masala

85g (3¹/₂oz) tomato sauce

1 tbsp tomato purée

1 tsp malt vinegar

1 tsp sugar

Place onions and potatoes in a 2-litre mixing bowl.

Add spices and bicarbonate of soda. Coat potatoes and onions.

Add a tbsp of flour to this, then gradually add water and flour until a good 'chip shop' batter is achieved.

Heat deep fat fryer with oil (this recipe may flavour oil so it is best to use separate oil for other foods).

When oil is hot, spoon mixture into it and cook each pakora for approximately 3 minutes until golden brown.

Put all chilli sauce ingredients in a mixer and blend until smooth.

Add water to dilute to desired consistency.

Serve the pakora immediately with salad and the chilli sauce.

Note This recipe is ideal for freezing. Chilli sauce can keep in an airtight jar in the refrigerator for a long time.

Vegetable Curry

Serves 4

Fry onion, garlic and chilli in a little oil until soft.

Add cumin seeds, ginger, turmeric and curry powder and cook gently for 2 minutes.

Add grated creamed coconut.

Once coconut has dissolved, add vegetable stock and stir into mixture.

Add carrots then courgettes and peppers at 5 minute intervals.

Finally, add cauliflower and simmer gently whilst stirring for 15–20 minutes.

Note A heavy-based pan is recommended for this recipe.

1 vegetable stock cube dissolved in 275ml (¹/₂ pint) water

1 medium onion, chopped

3 cloves of garlic, chopped

1 tsp turmeric

1 tsp cumin seeds

1 tsp fresh ginger, grated

1 tsp curry powder

¹/₄ block creamed coconut, grated

1 chilli (red or green), chopped

1 courgette, sliced

2 carrots, sliced

1 red pepper, sliced

1 medium cauliflower, broken into florets

1 medium-sized onion, chopped

6 eggs

2 medium-sized potatoes, thinly sliced and roughly chopped

olive oil

Tortilla Española

(Spanish omelette)

This is the staple fare of any tapas bar. Tortilla in Spain is very different from its Mexican namesake and looks more like a large potato cake. It can be eaten hot or cold, cut into wedges or bite-sized cubes (as an appetizer).

Serves 4–6

Heat 4 tablespoons of oil in a frying pan (the smaller the pan the thicker the omelette).

Sauté the onion in oil until it is soft.

Add the potatoes to the pan, add salt, and cook until they are soft, turning them so they do not stick (or use a non-stick pan).

Beat the eggs. Add the potatoes and onion to the beaten egg (there should be equal volumes of potato and egg). Add ground black pepper and some more salt if necessary.

Clean the frying pan and add enough oil to coat the bottom and sides lightly. Heat the oil and add the potato and egg mixture. Build up the mixture at the sides with a spatula or wooden spoon so that it forms a hard edge. If your pan is not non-stick, shake the pan from time to time to prevent the omelette sticking. When the mixture begins to set, place a plate the same diameter as the omelette on top of the mixture, quickly turn the pan upside down so that the half-cooked tortilla slides on to the plate, then return it to the pan on the heat so that the underside gets cooked. (If you do not feel up to this you can put the pan under a hot grill to cook the top, but this is cheating.)

Turn the tortilla out on to a plate. Cut into wedges and serve it like quiche.

Note This is the basic recipe for tortilla, but you can add flavours by cooking some red pepper, asparagus, chorizo, mushrooms, etc. with the potato and onion.

Aubergines and Courgettes

Courtesy of Giuliano's Ristorante, Edinburgh.

Serves 2

To make the tomato sauce, fry the garlic in the olive oil until soft, then add the tomatoes and mix well. Combine tomato sauce and pesto in a bowl.

Layer the grilled aubergine, then sauce mix, then courgette, then mozzarella in an ovenproof dish.

Follow this layer formation until you have reached the top of the dish.

Finish by sprinkling Parmesan cheese on top.

Cook for 5 minutes on 'High' in a microwave or in the oven for 15 minutes on a medium heat.

Garnish with a sprig of basil.

1 aubergine, sliced oblong and grilled
2 courgettes, sliced oblong and grilled
1 tbsp pesto
150g (5oz) mozzarella cheese, grated
Parmesan cheese to garnish, grated

Tomato Sauce

1 large can chopped tomatoes
2 cloves garlic, chopped
1 tbsp olive oil

Courgette Bread

A delicious recipe from a Nigerian friend.

Blend the contents of the two bowls and cook in a base-lined loaf tin at 180°C/350°F/Gas Mark 4 for 1 hour.

225g (8oz) courgettes, grated
1 large egg
6 tbsp demerara sugar
6 tbsp oil
Mix the above in one bowl and, in another, mix
175g (6oz) plain wholemeal flour
$1/_2$ tsp bicarbonate of soda
$1/_2$ tsp cinnamon
pinch of baking powder and salt
50g (2oz) nuts or raisins

Stuffed Marrow

With thanks to Alkmini Chaitow, who contributed this recipe from her own cookery book.

Serves 4–6

1 (approximately 1000g/32oz) large marrow, each end removed and emptied

280g (10oz) (2 cups) mixed ground nuts

2 eggs

1 tbsp (15ml) ginger purée

60g (2oz) (1 cup) dill and parsley, chopped

30g (1oz) ($^1/_2$ cup) spring onion, chopped

60g (2oz) ($^1/_2$ cup) pine kernels

230g (8oz) (2 cups) onion, chopped finely

85g (3oz) (1$^1/_2$ cups) wholemeal breadcrumbs

240g (3oz) (1 cup) olive/vegetable oil

pinch cayenne pepper

6 twists black pepper

salt substitute to taste

720g (20oz) (4 cups) sweet potatoes (optional)

US measures are given after imperial measures

Preheat oven to 200°C/400°F/Gas Mark 6.

Wash the marrow and remove 2cm (1") from each end (do not discard this) and then empty from the inside, and discard the part which contains the seeds, leaving the flesh intact.

Meanwhile, place half of the olive oil into a saucepan and lightly sauté the onions, spring onions, herbs and seasoning.

Remove from the heat and add in the ground nuts, pine kernels, breadcrumbs as well as the lightly beaten eggs. Mix all these ingredients thoroughly.

Using a spoon, stuff the mixture into the marrow, packing it firmly, and then replace the ends using wooden toothpicks to hold these in place. Remember to remove these after the cooking process and before serving.

Place the marrow into an oven container.

Optional

Peel and cut the sweet potatoes into 4cm (1$^1/_2$") lengths and pack these around the marrow.

Cover the contents with foil (for the first 30 minutes of the cooking process).

Pour the remainder of the olive oil into the container with 425ml (15 fl oz) (2 cups) of water and place this into the oven and allow to cook until all water has evaporated, remembering to remove the foil after 30 minutes.

Remove, take out the toothpicks, and serve hot or cold.

Savoy Cabbage

Courtesy of Giuliano's Ristorante, Edinburgh.

Serves 2

To make the tomato sauce, fry the garlic in the olive oil until soft, then add the tomatoes and mix well.

Fry onions, bacon and mushrooms in the olive oil and white wine.

Fill each cabbage leaf with this mixture, roll cabbage around filling and top with mozzarella, tomato sauce and, finally, the grated Parmesan.

Place under grill until cheese is golden.

Decorate with parsley.

---

4 Savoy cabbage leaves, blanched in very hot water

1 medium onion, chopped

6 medium mushrooms, chopped

4 rashers back bacon, chopped

1 tbsp olive oil

1 tbsp white wine

150g (5oz) mozzarella cheese

25g (1oz) Parmesan cheese, grated

Tomato Sauce

1 small can chopped tomatoes

2 cloves garlic, chopped

1 tbsp olive oil

Pasta and Vegetable Salad

Serves 4–6

1 tbsp oil

110g (4 oz) onion, finely chopped

1 level tbsp curry powder

150ml (¹/₄ pint) vegetable stock

2 level tbsp tomato purée

juice of half a lemon

4 level tbsp apricot jam

150ml (¹/₄ pint) mayonnaise or salad cream

450g–700g (1lb–1¹/₂lb) cooked pasta shells

seasoning

Fry the onions in the oil until soft and add the curry powder.

Stir in the stock, tomato purée, lemon juice and apricot jam.

Bring to the boil slowly and then simmer for 10 minutes. Allow to cool.

Stir in the mayonnaise or salad cream. Season to taste.

When cold, add the cooked pasta shells and fresh vegetables, e.g. mangetout, baby sweetcorn, peppers, mushrooms etc.

Note This dish can be turned into Coronation Chicken by simply replacing the vegetables with 450g (1lb) of cooked, diced chicken and adding a few sultanas.

150g (6oz) flat noodles

Basic Coating Sauce

25g (1oz) butter

25g (1oz) plain flour

250ml (¹/₂ pint) milk

200g (8oz) Cheddar cheese, finely grated

200g (8oz) carrots, sliced and cooked

200g (8oz) peas, cooked

salt and pepper

4 eggs, hard-boiled

chopped parsley

Noodle Nest

Serves 4

Cook noodles in boiling salted water according to directions.

Drain and arrange in ring on a warm dish. Keep hot.

Make basic coating sauce by melting butter, adding flour, then slowly adding milk.

Bring to the boil, stirring, then add 150g (6oz) of the cheese. Add carrots and peas. Season to taste.

Halve the hard-boiled eggs.

Pour sauce mixture into noodle ring. Arrange hardboiled eggs on top.

Sprinkle with the remaining cheese mixed with some chopped parsley. Serve at once.

Vegetarian Stir Fry

Quantities depend on servings required.

Heat wok and add oil. Test temperature of oil by dropping in a piece of ginger. If this sizzles vigorously, it's ready.

Add ginger, garlic and onion heads, together with nuts.

Cook for 30 seconds, then add remainder of vegetables.

Cook for approximately 1 minute (longer for large quantities).

Add lemon juice, sherry and soy sauce, and cook for a further minute.

Finally, add mangoes and heat until warm.

Serve with brown rice.

mushrooms, cut into short strips

carrots, cut into short strips

celery, cut into short strips

courgettes, cut into short strips

spring onions, separated into white 'heads' finely chopped and green 'tails' cut into 2" lengths

cashew nuts

fresh root ginger, finely chopped

fresh garlic, finely chopped

mango, fresh or tinned

lemon juice

dry sherry

light soy sauce

groundnut oil

Optional

baby sweetcorn

peppers

Vegetables

Rösti *(Swiss potato cake)*

Serves 3–4

Heat butter in a heavy based frying pan. Add onion and cook without browning for 2–3 minutes.

Add potatoes, season well and fry over a fairly high heat, turning all the time until golden brown.

Lower heat, press potatoes well down and continue to cook until a crust forms underneath.

Turn out on a warm plate, so that the brown crust is uppermost. Sprinkle with chopped parsley. Serve cut into wedges.

900g (2lb) potatoes, boiled in jackets until just tender, cooled, peeled, then roughly grated

75g (3oz) butter

1 medium-sized onion, finely chopped

salt and pepper

chopped parsley to garnish

Sunday Carrots

Lovely with the Sunday roast and, of course, at Christmas with the turkey.

Serves 4

Put everything in a pan and simmer until tender (about 30 minutes).

450g (1lb) carrots, scrubbed and cut into evenly sized lengths

juice ¹/₂ lemon

2 tsp dill weed, chopped

2 tsp honey

2 tsp water

salt and pepper

Mrs Cox's Pots

Preheat oven to 150°C/300°F/Gas Mark 2.

Place the potatoes in an ovenproof dish.

Fry bacon in hot oil until brown.

Add the onion and cook until soft.

Pour the stock into the pan with the bacon and onion. Simmer for 1 minute.

Add salt and black pepper.

Pour this over the potatoes and bake in the top of the oven (uncovered) for 1 hour or until the potatoes are cooked.

4 large potatoes, peeled and sliced

1 beef or chicken stock cube, dissolved in 275ml (1/2 pint) hot water

4 rashers bacon, cut into small pieces

1 large onion, chopped

salt and black pepper to taste

Maryland Potatoes

Serves 4

Preheat oven to 180°C/350°F/Gas Mark 4.

Place potatoes in a buttered casserole with the sweetcorn and salt and pepper.

Pour over just enough hot milk to cover.

Put into oven on top shelf and cook for 1/2 hour or until potatoes are soft. Remove from oven.

Place rashers of bacon on top then continue baking until bacon is brown and crisp.

Finish off under grill if necessary.

700g (1 1/2 lb) potatoes, cut into 1cm (1/2") cubes

10g (1/2 oz) butter

1 small can sweetcorn kernels

salt and pepper

275–425ml (1/2–3/4 pint) hot milk

5–6 rashers streaky bacon

New Potato Salad with Vinaigrette

Ideal accompaniment for salmon dishes.

Boil potatoes for 15 minutes or until just tender.

Measure balsamic vinaigrette into a salad bowl and add herbs and onion.

Drain the potatoes and toss into the bowl with the dressing and seasoning.

450g (1lb) new potatoes
3–4 tbsp balsamic vinaigrette
1 × 20g packet fresh herbs for fish, finely chopped (or alternatively use a combination of fresh herbs, such as dill, chives and parsley)
1 medium-sized red onion, thinly sliced
salt and pepper

Potato Salad Log Party Treats

Season the potatoes with salt, pepper and mustard.

Place on a damp cloth (or aluminium foil).

Roll out to form rectangle shape approximately 1/2" thick.

Blend together the mayonnaise, cream cheese and sour cream. Then add the eggs, onions, peppers and celery, and add to the mayonnaise mixture.

Spread the mixture over the potato and roll up.

Refrigerate for at least 1 hour, then cut into 1" thick slices and serve.

450g (1lb) potatoes, mashed
1 tsp mustard
1/3 cup (approximately 60g; 2.5oz) mayonnaise
75g (3oz) cream cheese
1 tbsp sweet pickle relish
1/4 cup (approximately 50g; 2oz) sour cream
4 hard-boiled eggs, chopped
2 tbsp onions, finely chopped
2 tbsp peppers, finely chopped
2 tbsp celery, finely chopped

Scalloped Potatoes with Goat Cheese and Herbes de Provence

1¹/₂ cups (350ml; 12 fl oz) whipping cream

1¹/₂ cups (350ml; 12 fl oz) canned chicken broth

1 cup (220ml; 8 fl oz) dry white wine

¹/₂ cup (110g; 4oz) minced shallots

1 tbsp minced garlic (roasted garlic spread is also recommended)

4 tsp herbes de Provence (a blend of basil, thyme, rosemary, oregano and lavender)

³/₄ tsp salt

1 × 275/315g (10oz/11oz) bar fresh goat cheese, crumbled

1.8kg (4lb) russet (baking) potatoes

This is an excellent side-dish to serve with roast beef. Makes the house smell heavenly while it's cooking.

Preheat oven to 200°C/400°F/Gas Mark 6.

Butter a 32 × 23 × 5cm (13 × 9 × 2″) glass baking dish. Peel potatoes and slice very thinly, using a mandoline or food processor slicing blade.

Mix the first seven ingredients in a large pot and bring to a simmer over medium-high heat.

Add half the cheese and whisk until smooth, keeping the remaining cheese in the refrigerator.

Add potatoes to the pot; bring to a simmer.

Transfer potato mixture to the prepared baking dish and spread evenly.

Cover with foil and bake for 15 minutes. Uncover and continue baking until potatoes are very tender and the liquid bubbles thickly, about 50 minutes.

Dot potatoes with remaining crumbled cheese and return to the oven for approximately 5 more minutes until cheese melts.

Allow to cool for 15 minutes before serving.

450g (1lb) button onions

25g (1oz) sugar

50g (2oz) butter

Glazed Onions

Boil onions in their skins for 10 minutes then plunge into cold water. Peel.

Heat sugar and butter in a heavy-based pan.

Add onions and cook, stirring occasionally, for about 5 minutes until the onions are golden and tender.

Tomato Rice

Heat oil in large saucepan. Stir in rice then pour in hot chicken stock, tomato ketchup and sugar.

Simmer for 12 minutes or until tender, stirring occasionally, then add peas and salad onions.

Cook for a further 5 minutes until peas are tender.

Drain and serve with curry.

225g (8oz) long grain rice
1 tbsp sesame oil
750ml (1¼ pints) hot chicken stock
4 tbsp tomato ketchup
1 tbsp sugar
75g (3oz) frozen peas
3 salad onions, chopped

Hot Rice

Ideal served cold in a buffet or at a barbeque!

Place oil, lemon juice, garlic, chillies, soy sauce, hoisin sauce, honey, vinegar and seasoning in a large bowl and mix well.

Add hot rice, together with remaining ingredients, and mix well.

Serve hot or cold.

4 tbsp sesame oil
juice of 1 lemon
1 clove garlic, peeled and crushed
2 (or more!) dried red chillies, deseeded and crushed
2 tbsp soy sauce
1 tbsp hoisin sauce
1 tbsp clear honey
2 tbsp wine vinegar
salt and pepper to taste
350g (12oz) brown rice, cooked and hot
4 spring onions, thinly sliced
225g (8oz) can pineapple pieces, in juice
225g (8oz) beansprouts
2 small peppers (red/green), sliced
50g (2oz) raisins
50g (2oz) cashew nuts, toasted
2 tbsp sesame seeds, toasted
50g (2oz) unsalted peanuts

Carrot Salad

225g (8oz) carrots, trimmed, peeled and coarsely grated

$^1/_4$ tsp salt

1 tbsp vegetable oil

$^1/_2$ tsp whole black mustard seeds

$^1/_2$ tsp lemon juice

1 green chilli, cut into long thin slices

Heat oil in a very small pan over a medium heat.

When very hot, add the mustard seeds and cover with lid.

When they begin to 'pop', add carrots, salt, lemon juice and chilli.

Stir for 1 minute on low heat, cool then serve.

1 bunch of spinach (or silver beef), washed, dried and de-stalked

2 hard boiled eggs, chopped

2 bacon rashers, cooked and chopped

1 tbsp almonds (or salted peanuts), toasted and chopped

$^1/_2$ cup (115g; 4 fl oz) French dressing (olive/walnut oil and wine vinegar or lemon juice with added crushed garlic clove)

2 tbsp spring onions or chives, chopped

Spinach Salad

Serves 4

Break spinach into bite-size pieces.

Place in bowl with eggs.

Toss with dressing.

Sprinkle with bacon, nuts and onions.

Trio of Melons

Courtesy of Denis Zominy, Senior Sous Chef,
Marriott Dalmahoy.

Serves 10

Make stock syrup by quartering oranges and lemons and boiling with the sugar, water and cinnamon stick.

Leave to cool, then chill.

Add saffron and seeds of passion fruit.

Parisienne the melons with a 12mm scoop. Layer the melon balls in a metal pipe approximately 50–60mm in height. Push melon in gently to extract some liquid but do not push too hard as you will squash the melon balls.

Put a level layer of crème fraîche on top of the melon.

Chill for approximately 35 minutes if possible.

Remove metal pipe and garnish top of melon with strawberries, raspberries, blackberries and physalis.

Place in centre of plate and drizzle syrup round the melon and garnish with fresh berries.

1 cantaloupe melon
1 galia melon
1 honeydew melon
500g (1lb 2oz) crème fraîche
1 punnet strawberries
1 punnet raspberries
1 punnet blackberries or blueberries
10 physalis
1 pkt mint

Stock Syrup

2 oranges
2 lemons
500g (1lb 2oz) sugar
570ml (1 pint) water
1 cinnamon stick
pinch of saffron
6 passion fruits

French Apple Crumble

Serves 6

450g (1lb) cooking apples, peeled

225g (8oz) plain flour

110g (4oz) butter

110g (4oz) sugar

2 tsps baking powder

vanilla essence/ cinnamon/nuts/raisins to flavour (optional)

Preheat oven to 200°C/400°F/Gas Mark 6.

Mix flour and sugar in a bowl. Add the butter (use the butter straight from the refrigerator – it can be grated into the flour and sugar mix).

Rub mixture through fingers until it resembles breadcrumbs. Add the baking powder and vanilla essence to the dry mixture.

Spread half the mixture across a 23cm (9") flan dish.

Grate the apple onto the dry mixture to form a second layer (if you are careful you can grate the apple without coring it but watch your fingers!).

Add nuts, raisins, cinnamon etc. to the apple mixture. Spread the remaining dry crumble mix to form a third layer.

Bake for approximately 45 minutes. (The cooking time will vary with the thickness of the crumble.)

Serve with crème fraîche, crème anglaise or ice cream.

825g (30oz) canned peaches

2 tsp lemon juice

1/4 cup peach syrup (from can)

6 tbsp plain or wholemeal flour

6 tbsp sugar

1/8 tsp nutmeg

1/4 tsp cinnamon

3 tbsp butter or oil

Peach Crumble

Preheat oven to 190°C/375°F/Gas Mark 5.

Spread peaches in greased casserole dish. Mix lemon juice and syrup and pour over peaches.

Mix together flour, sugar, nutmeg and cinnamon.

Lightly work in butter with fork until mixture is crumbly and sprinkle over peaches.

Bake for 30 minutes or until brown and crispy.

Serve warm with ice cream or custard.

As an alternative, you can use half of the peach syrup with 3 tbsp peach schnapps or rum.

Cyclists' Pudding

Serves 4–6 or 3 hungry cyclists!

Preheat oven to 180°C/350°F/Gas Mark 4.

Lightly butter a deep baking dish (1½ litre/3 pint capacity).

Spoon the syrup over the bottom of the dish.

Remove the crusts from the bread, butter the slices and cut into fingers or triangles.

Place buttered side up in the baking dish, sprinkling a few raisins/sultanas in between the layers.

Whisk the milk with the eggs and pour on top of the bread, and bake for 40–50 minutes.

(Once prepared, the pudding can sit for an hour before baking if desired.)

This pudding rises like a soufflé so should be served immediately with vanilla ice cream or crème fraîche.

60ml (4 tbsp) golden syrup
8 medium slices of bread (**not** sliced bread)
50g (2oz) spreadable butter or margarine
2 beaten eggs
50g (2oz) sultanas or raisins
425ml (³/₄ pint) milk

Florence Lower Benkert's Open Fruit Pie

A Pennsylvanian recipe.

Serves 8

Preheat oven to 180°C/350°F/Gas Mark 4.

Beat egg, sugar, cornflour, and salt together. Add butter. Add juice (if any) from fruit. Put fruit in pastry case and pour mixture over.

Dust cinnamon on the top and bake for 50 minutes until custard is done, i.e. until bubbles form in centre.

¹/₂ cup sugar
1 egg
2 tbsp melted butter
1 tbsp cornstarch (cornflour)
pinch salt
4 cups or more of fresh fruit (blueberries are recommended)
1 uncooked shortcrust pastry case

Steamed Syrup Pudding

Serves 4

4 tbsp golden syrup

175g (6oz) butter

75g (3oz) caster sugar

75g (3oz) light brown sugar

25g (1oz) white breadcrumbs

25g (1oz) sultanas

2 large eggs

2 tbsp milk

175g (6oz) self-raising flour

Butter a large pudding basin (2 pint) and pour in the golden syrup, sultanas and breadcrumbs.

Cream together the butter and sugar.

Whisk the eggs in a separate bowl and add them, a little at a time, to the butter mixture, mixing until well blended.

Gently stir in the flour and spoon the mixture into the pudding basin.

Cut a piece of greaseproof paper (2" or 3") larger than the diameter of the basin top and make a couple of folds which will allow the mixture to rise. Put the paper over the top of the mixture and secure round the bowl with string.

Cover the greaseproof paper with a piece of aluminium foil, again pleated and secured with string.

Place the basin on top of a pastry cutter in a large saucepan to keep the base of the basin off the bottom of the pan.

Fill the pan with boiling water to halfway up the basin. Cover with a lid and simmer for 90 minutes. Check every 20 minutes or so to make sure the water has not boiled dry (top up with boiling water as necessary).

After 90 minutes, remove the pan from heat and allow to cool slightly. Carefully remove the basin from the water and leave to sit for 5 minutes.

Remove the foil and greaseproof paper (beware of steam) and turn the pudding onto a warmed serving dish.

Serve whilst still warm with whipped cream or a scoop of butterscotch ice cream.

Baked Rice Pudding

Serves 2–3

Preheat oven to 190°C/375°F/Gas Mark 5.

Put rice in a pudding dish. Cover with ¹/₂ cup water and cook in the oven until the water has been absorbed. Add milk, sugar, butter and raisins. Stir and put back in oven.

Stir now and again and add more milk if necessary.

Cook for about 2 hours until it has a brown, crisp skin. Delicious!

30ml (3 dsp) pudding rice
20ml (2 dsp) sugar
2 cups milk
¹/₂ cup water
4 knobs butter
1 handful raisins

Christmas Plum Pudding

Prepare fruit.

Sift flour, baking powder, salt and spices into bowl with fruit. Rub in suet, stir in other ingredients and add liquid last.

Grease bowl, cover with greased paper and boil for 6 hours.

Cool and leave for 6 weeks.

Steam for 3 hours when required.

110g (4oz) sultanas
110g (4oz) currants
110g (4oz) plain flour
25g (1oz) brown sugar
8 chopped prunes
110g (4oz) grated potato
¹/₂ tsp mixed spice
¹/₂ tsp baking powder
pinch of salt
110g (4oz) raisins
50g (2oz) mixed peel
110g (4oz) Atora suet
1 tbsp treacle
110g (4oz) grated carrot
50g (2oz) chopped almonds
¹/₂ tsp grated nutmeg
grated rind of 1 lemon
2 tbsp of brandy

Carrot Pudding

A dessert from India.

Serves 4–6

1kg (2lb 4oz) carrots

1 litre (1³/₄ pints) full cream milk

150g (5oz) sugar

1 tbsp unsalted butter

110g (4oz) raisins

small amount of chopped unroasted cashew nuts (optional)

Scrape and grate carrots and put into pan with milk.

Boil slowly until all of the milk has evaporated.

Mix in sugar followed by the unsalted butter.

Heat on a low temperature for 10 minutes, stirring continuously.

Remove from heat and add raisins (and cashew nuts).

Serve while hot.

Clootie Dumpling

450g (1lb) self-raising flour

225g (8oz) granulated sugar

1 tsp bicarbonate of soda

1 tbsp treacle

water to mix

450g (1lb) mixed fruit

175g (6oz) suet

¹/₂ tsp salt

3 tsp mixed spice

Mix all ingredients together in a large bowl and add enough water to give a soft consistency.

Sprinkle a square muslin cloth with a good coating of flour and drop the mixture onto the floured cloth.

Tie securely leaving room for expansion.

Place on an upturned plate in a large pan of boiling water.

Boil steadily for 4 hours, keeping a check on the water level.

Cool on a plate for a few minutes, then peel off cloth very gently.

Dry off in a cool oven for 10 minutes.

Cathie's Krummeltorte

Cathie's husband, David, believes a dessert should only be a pudding! Hence one of her many recipes for puds!

Preheat oven to 220°C/425°F/Gas Mark 7.

Grease loose-bottomed sandwich tin.

Cut apples into pieces and simmer in pan with half of sugar (no water) and vanilla essence.

Rub margarine into flour with remaining sugar. Mix to dough consistency with the egg.

Spread two-thirds of mixture into tin and press down slightly. Top with apples. Spread rest of mixture on top.

Bake for 25 minutes.

To serve, sprinkle with caster sugar.

450g (1lb) apples
110g (4oz) caster sugar
275g (10oz) self-raising flour
75g (3oz) margarine
1 egg
1 tsp vanilla essence

Malakoff Torte

An incredibly rich, classic Austrian torte.

Cream butter and egg yolks until fluffy. Add sugar, almonds and brandy. Fold in whipped cream.

Line sides and base of round, deep-sided, loose-bottomed 20–23cm (8–9") cake tin with non-stick paper.

Arrange a layer of sponge fingers on base of tin, breaking them up where necessary.

Top with half of the cream mixture. Add another layer of sponge fingers.

Smooth remaining mixture over top and refrigerate for at least 2 hours.

150g (5oz) unsalted butter
4 egg yolks
150g (5oz) icing sugar, sieved
150g (5oz) ground almonds
1 tbsp brandy
275ml (1/2 pint) whipped cream
approximately 30 sponge fingers

Banoffi Pie

Serves 4–6

1 can condensed milk

1 large banana

175g (6oz) digestive biscuits, crushed

275ml (½ pint) double/whipping cream

75g (3oz) butter

½ tsp sugar

1 tsp Camp coffee (optional)

Melt butter in saucepan and add biscuits to make base. Line base and sides of flan dish with mixture.

Place unopened can of condensed milk on its side in a pan of boiling water (ensure the can is covered with the water). Boil for 4 hours taking care not to let pan boil dry.

Spoon the contents of the can onto the base – if the milk has not caramelized evenly, simply mix together and pass through a sieve onto the base.

Allow to cool and slice the banana onto the toffee base.

Mix the sugar and the coffee into the double or whipping cream – ensure the cream is nice and thick – and spoon over the banana. Chill the finished pie and decorate.

150g (¼ pint) fromage frais

1 punnet strawberries, chopped

1 banana, chopped

150g (¼ pint) natural yoghurt

2 tbsp honey

25g (1oz) hazelnuts, crushed

chocolate powder (to decorate)

Coppa Giuliano

Recommended by Giuliano's Ristorante, Edinburgh: they tell us children will love it – we believe them!

Serves 2

Mix all ingredients (except chocolate powder) in a bowl until thick and creamy.

Spoon into sundae dishes, dust with chocolate powder and top each dish with a strawberry.

Chocolate Orange Roulade

Serves 4–6

Grease and line a Swiss-roll tray with silicone paper.

Melt the chocolate in a microwave oven or over a pan of hot water.

Whisk the egg yolks and the caster sugar until pale and fluffy.

Allow the chocolate to cool slightly then add to the egg yolk and sugar mixture.

Whisk the egg whites until stiff and fold them into the chocolate mixture.

Turn the mixture into the Swiss-roll tray and bake at 190°C/375°F/Gas Mark 5 for 15–20 minutes until set and cracks begin to appear on top.

Cover the tray with a dampened tea towel and seal with cling film. Leave to cool for at least 3 hours.

Put greaseproof paper the same size as the tray on a flat surface and sprinkle with caster sugar.

After removing the cling film and tea towel, turn the baked roulade out onto the paper and peel off the silicone.

Whisk the cream (not too stiff) and add the Cointreau.

Spread the Cointreau/cream over the roulade base, then roll up the base, short end to short end.

Sprinkle with icing sugar and grated Terry's Chocolate Orange.

175g (6oz) dark, high quality chocolate

5 med eggs, separated

175g (6oz) caster sugar

275ml (10 fl oz) double cream

Cointreau to taste (say 55ml (1–2 fl oz))

Decoration

Bar of Terry's Chocolate Orange

Icing sugar

Marquise au Chocolat

Courtesy of Michel Bouyer, L'Auberge Restaurant, Edinburgh.

Serves 6

150g (6oz) good-quality, dark, bitter cooking chocolate

1 dsp (10ml) very strong coffee

100g (4oz) butter, unsalted

2 eggs, separated

80g (3oz) icing sugar

Whisk whites until stiff. Add sugar. Whisk again until stiff.

Put chocolate, coffee and butter in a bowl over hot water and stir well until melted. Add yolks and mix.

Fold chocolate mixture into egg whites and put into loaf tin lined with cling film.

Leave in refrigerator overnight.

Serve sliced with strawberries or cream sauce.

Choc Nut Sundae

ice cream (vanilla or chocolate, or both)

chopped mixed nuts

meringue (individual meringue nests are recommended)

banana (optional), sliced

chocolate sauce

Serves 1

Take a sundae glass, the taller the better.

Crush the meringue to form a layer at the bottom of the glass.

Add some chopped nuts, a dob of ice cream and some sliced banana.

Create similar layers to the top of the glass.

Add a generous helping of chocolate sauce and sprinkle chopped nuts on top.

Create different sundaes using any other types of fruit, sauce and flavours of ice cream.

Fresh fruit gives a better result.

Chocolate Marshmallow Delight

Serves 6

Melt butter and add biscuits. Mix thoroughly. Press into a flan dish. Cook for 8 minutes in a moderate oven. Cool and then put in refrigerator.

Put chocolate into a large bowl over a pan of hot water and melt.

Add marshmallows and keep mixing as they melt.

Add brandy and vanilla essence.

Beat mixture with a wooden spoon and then allow to cool.

Whip double cream and fold into mixture.

Pour on top of biscuit base.

Put back in refrigerator for about an hour.

Decorate with almonds and/or crushed chocolate flake.

18/20 chocolate digestive biscuits, crushed

110g (4oz) butter or margarine

400g (14oz) grated chocolate

22 marshmallows

2 tbsp brandy

1 tsp vanilla essence

225ml (8 fl oz) double cream

chocolate flake/flaked almonds for decoration

Rich Chocolate Mousse

Serves 3–4

110g (4oz) plain dessert chocolate

2 eggs, separated

1 tbsp rum or brandy

Break chocolate into small squares.

Melt in basin over pan of hot water barely simmering. Make sure bottom of bowl is not touching water in pan. When smooth, remove from heat.

Beat egg yolks and add to chocolate while still hot. Beat together very thoroughly.

Add rum or brandy a little at a time, beating well.

Leave mixture to cool for about 15 minutes.

Beat egg whites to soft peak stage.

Fold into chocolate mixture.

Spoon into large dish or several small dishes.

Cover with aluminium foil or clingfilm.

Leave overnight or chill in refrigerator for 2 hours.

425ml (³/₄ pint) double cream

110ml (4 fl oz) brandy

100g (3¹/₂ oz) ginger marmalade

Ginger Syllabub

Whip cream and brandy together until it just holds its shape.

Fold in ginger marmalade and chill thoroughly (preferably overnight).

Serve in medium wine glasses on top of diced fresh melon or poached pears/tinned pear segments.

Whisky and Honey Ice Cream

Serves 4

Add whisky and melted honey to egg yolks, and whisk. Fold in cream (whipped to a floppy state).

Pour contents into individual ramekins or a container suitable for freezer. Freeze for a minimum 6 hours.

Serve directly from freezer (alcohol content keeps it softish!).

4 tbsp honey
4 egg yolks
4 tbsp whisky
275g (10oz) whipping cream

Ice Cream

Beat cream and vanilla until stiff. Fold in condensed milk and freeze.

Other flavourings can be added, e.g. grated chocolate, fruit purée such as strawberries, raspberries or mango, rum and raisins, coffee and almonds.

570ml (1 pint) whipping cream
1 can sweetened condensed milk
vanilla essence

Buried Strawberries

Serves 4

Beat the cream until stiff, then mix the yoghurt into it. Beat the egg white stiffly and fold it into the cream mixture.

Stir in the sugar and pour the mixture over the fruit.

Put the dish in the refrigerator for about an hour before serving.

450g (1lb) fresh strawberries
150ml (¼ pint) double cream
1 small carton natural yoghurt
1 egg white
2 tbsp caster sugar

Mauritian Forest Fruit

Serves 4

350g (12 oz) raspberries (or other forest berries)

275ml (10 fl oz) double cream

275ml (10 fl oz) Greek yoghurt

2 tbsp dark Muscovado sugar

Put the berries in one large dish or split into smaller individual dishes and sprinkle with 1 tbsp of the sugar.

Whip the cream (not too stiff) and fold into the yoghurt.

Spread the mixture over the berries then sprinkle the remaining sugar over the top.

Chill for at least 4 hours before serving.

Forest Fruits Italiano

Courtesy of Giuliano's Ristorante, Edinburgh

Serves 2

200g (7oz) mixed forest fruits

250g (9oz) mascarpone cheese

4 Amaretti biscuits, crushed

25g (1oz) flaked almonds

25g (1oz) chocolate sauce

pinch of icing sugar (to decorate)

Mix mascarpone cheese and chocolate sauce, then pour into sundae dishes.

Add the forest fruits and place Amaretti biscuits and flaked almonds on top of fruit.

Decorate with one whole Amaretti biscuit and icing sugar.

Fruits of the Forest Brûlé

Mix together the fruits of the forest and the pie filling and place in the bottom of a dish.

Whip cream, fold in yoghurt and pile mixture on top of fruit.

Sprinkle the creamy topping with a layer of soft brown sugar and place under a hot grill until it caramelizes.

Note For best results, make the day before and refrigerate.

1 pkt frozen fruits of the forest

1 can Morton's red/black cherry pie filling

275ml (^{1}/$_2$ pint) double cream

275ml (^{1}/$_2$ pint) Greek yoghurt

Pears in White Wine

Serves 4

Peel the pears, leaving the stalks on.

Slice a small portion from the base so that they stand upright.

Squeeze the orange and make up to 150ml (^{1}/$_4$ pint) by adding orange juice from a carton.

Put the wine, juice, orange rind and sugar in a pan and bring to the boil.

Add the peeled pears and poach them gently for 20 minutes.

Remove pears from the pan and stand them in a serving dish.

Boil the remaining juice until it turns syrupy, then spoon it over the pears.

Chill thoroughly and serve with whipped cream.

4 pears (Williams or Comice, ready to eat preferably)

grated rind and juice of an orange

25g (1oz) demerara sugar

150ml (^{1}/$_4$ pint) white wine

150ml (^{1}/$_4$ pint) orange juice

Cranachan

Courtesy of Caledonian Hotel, Edinburgh

Serves 4

570ml (1 pint) double cream

150ml (¹/₄ pint) whisky

225g (8oz) oatcakes, crushed

225g (8oz) fresh raspberries

25ml (1 fl oz) Scotch honey

Whip cream, whisky and honey until lightly peaked.

Purée raspberries (keep 4 to garnish).

Mix oatcakes into the cream mixture.

Place 1 tbsp of puréed raspberries into serving glasses and pipe cream mixture on top.

Decorate each glass with a raspberry and a pinch of crushed oats.

50g (2oz) pinhead oatmeal

275ml (¹/₂ pint) double cream

25–50g (1–2oz) caster sugar (or to taste)

110g (4oz) fresh raspberries

generous measure of whisky/rum or vanilla essence

McCranachan

Serves 2

Toast oatmeal lightly in a thick-bottomed frying pan over a gentle heat, or in oven.

Beat cream until frothy but not stiff. Sweeten to taste.

Mix in the oatmeal and flavour with whisky/rum or vanilla.

Wash and sieve the raspberries, stir into the cream mixture and serve.

Pineapple Pavlova

Set oven at 120°C/250°F/Gas Mark $\frac{1}{2}$, but turn down to 110°C/225°F/Gas Mark $\frac{1}{4}$ when pavlova is put into oven.

Beat egg whites until stiff. Add caster sugar and beat a little.

Add cornflour, vinegar and water mixture and beat until stiff.

Spread mixture onto an inverted Swiss-roll tray lined with silicone paper (i.e. turn the tray upside down as this will make it much easier to serve the meringue).

Bake for $1\frac{1}{2}$ hours and leave in oven until cool.

When cold, place an oblong plate over the meringue and turn it over so that the underside is uppermost. Peel off the silicone paper.

Pineapple Cream

Lightly whip the double cream (not too much).

Drain pineapple and fold into whipped cream. Add a little sugar to taste.

Spread pineapple cream onto pavlova covering the whole area.

Decoration Suggestions

Toasted flaked almonds, fresh fruit, grated chocolate etc.

Pavlova

3 egg whites

175g (6oz) caster sugar

1 tsp cornflour
1 tsp vinegar
1 tsp water
(mix together)

Pineapple Cream

250 ml ($\frac{1}{2}$ pint) double cream

can crushed pineapple

caster sugar

Amaretto Cream

Courtesy of Denis Zominy, Senior Sous Chef, Marriott Dalmahoy.

Serves 10

1 small bottle amaretto liqueur

6tbsp almond essence

200g (7oz) flaked almonds, roasted

50 small Amaretti biscuits or macaroons

2 whole eggs

350g (12oz) mascarpone cheese

400g (14oz) double cream, whipped

10g (¹/₂oz) gelatine

250g (9oz) caster sugar

10 tea cups for serving

Put eggs in a heat-resistant glass bowl (metal will do) with 150g (5oz) of the caster sugar.

Whisk egg and sugar mixture over a pan of simmering hot water (big enough to allow the bowl to touch the water so that the heat can get to the mixture). Whisk until mixture is very creamy.

Dissolve the gelatine in warm water and add to the mixture – do this while the mixture is still on the heat so that the gelatine dissolves completely.

Take the mixture off the heat and let it cool slightly before continuing.

When cool enough, add the mascarpone cheese (ensure mixture is cool enough so that the cream does not melt).

Whisk the remainder of the caster sugar into whipped cream and add to mixture along with almond essence and amaretto liqueur (to taste).

Take each cup and fill by a third. Put 2 Amaretti biscuits and a teaspoon of liqueur in each cup, then fill the remainder of cup. Decorate top with flaked almonds and put in refrigerator to set for at least 3 hours.

Serve with the rest of the biscuits and a small liqueur glass of amaretto.

American Cheesecake

Serves 8–12

Preheat oven to 180°C/350°F/Gas Mark 4.

Use a springform tin (approximately 23cm (9")) diameter).

To make base Crush biscuits until they are very small crumbs. Add melted butter/margarine and mix well. Press into springform tin and set aside.

To make filling Whip the cream cheese until light and fluffy. Add the eggs, sugar and vanilla and whip again until smooth. Pour over top of base.

Bake for 45 minutes or until the top is brown and cracked. Take out of the oven, pour the sour cream over the cheesecake and return to the oven for 5 minutes.

Allow to cool thoroughly. Before releasing the springs at the side of the tin, run a sharp knife around the sides of the cheesecake.

Decorate with strawberries, raspberries, kiwis or other fresh soft fruit.

Note It is best eaten cold from the refrigerator.

Base

Digestive biscuits (approx. ¹/₂ large packet)

Butter/margarine (approx. 4 tbsp)

Filling

4 pkts cream cheese (250g each)

4 eggs

225g (8oz) sugar

1¹/₂ tsp vanilla

Topping

1 large container of sour cream (or crème fraîche)

Anne's Easy Lemon Cheesecake

Serves 6

Mix biscuits with butter. Spoon into pie plate or flan dish to make a base. Chill to harden.

Melt jelly in boiling water. Cool.

Beat cream cheese with caster sugar and sour cream until smooth and blended.

Whisk in jelly. Fold in double cream.

100g (4oz) crushed digestive biscuits

50g (2oz) melted butter

1 pkt lemon jelly

150ml (¹/₄ pint) boiling water

225g (8oz) cream cheese (Philadelphia is recommended)

50g (2oz) caster sugar

150ml (¹/₄ pint) sour cream

275ml (¹/₂ pint) double cream, whipped

Banana & Apricot Dessert

A dessert that is not too wicked for dieters and very quick to prepare. Also a good way to use up bananas that are nearing the end of their shelf life.

Serves 2

2 or 3 bananas

small can of apricot halves in juice (not syrup)

lemon juice

brown sugar to taste (1 scant tbsp should be sufficient)

Slice the bananas into an ovenproof dish or saucepan. Squeeze lemon juice over bananas to stop them going brown.

Add the apricots, juice and sugar. These can be cooked either in the microwave for about 3–4 minutes depending on power, or in a pan long enough for the bananas to cook without breaking down.

Serve immediately.

Alternatively, the mixture can be cooked down, then mashed or liquidized, and served with a swirl of cream on top or with tiny meringues for a more glamorous presentation.

Lemon Nothings

A light and fluffy tangy pudding.

3 eggs

3oz sugar

juice of one lemon

rind of one lemon, finely grated

Separate the eggs.

Beat egg yolks and sugar together, then add the lemon juice and rind.

Gently heat in a heavy pan till the mixture thickens (do not allow to boil), stirring constantly.

Allow to cool.

Whisk the egg whites until stiff and fold into the egg yolk mixture.

Divide between dessert glasses and refrigerate.

Serve with ice cream/whipped cream and wafers.

Chinese Imperial

Serves 4–6

Dip biscuits in coffee mixture and use to layer base of dish.

Spread top with half of the ginger preserve into which has been mixed 2 tbsp coffee mixture.

Cover with half of whipped cream.

Create further layers using the rest of the ingredients, finishing with the whipped cream.

Decorate with any of the following:

chocolate flake (crumbled), almonds (slivered), chocolate (grated), walnuts (crushed).

Chill in refrigerator until ready to serve.

2 pkt small size ginger nut biscuits
half a jar ginger preserve
150ml (5 fl oz) whipping cream
2 tbsp instant coffee (dissolved in 275ml (10 fl oz) boiling water)
4 tbsp brandy (add to coffee)

Lemon Crunch

Lemon Cream

1 can condensed milk
2 lemons
150g (5oz) single cream

Beat condensed milk, lemon juice and rind of lemons together. Mix in cream and set aside.

Melt the butter and mix with the biscuits and sugar to a crumbly consistency. Sprinkle onto the lemon mixture. Refrigerate until required.

Note Do not freeze.

Crunch

1 pkt digestive biscuits, finely crushed
50g (2oz) butter
small amount brown sugar

Lemon Cake

Preheat oven to 180°C/350°F/Gas Mark 4.

Cream sugar and margarine, then beat in the eggs one by one.

Add the flour, grated rind of both lemons and the juice of one lemon.

Turn the mixture into two 18cm (7") round sandwich tins and bake for 30 to 40 minutes.

For the icing, mix the sugar with a small knob of soft margarine and the juice of the remaining lemon.

110g (4oz) margarine

225g (8oz) sugar

4 eggs

175g (6oz) brown self-raising flour

2 lemons

225g (8oz) icing sugar

lemon juice

175g (6oz) self-raising flour, plus a little extra

175g (6oz) butter, plus some for greasing cake tin

175g (6oz) caster sugar

2 large or 3 small eggs

finely grated zest of 1 large lemon

3–4 tbsp milk

Syrup

75g (3oz) caster sugar

juice of 1 large lemon

Topping

125g (4oz) sifted icing sugar

1–2 tbsp lemon juice

Lemon Drizzle Cake

Preheat oven to 180°C/350°/Gas Mark 4.

Grease and flour a 900g (2lb) loaf tin. Sift flour into large bowl, add remaining cake ingredients and beat until soft and light. Spoon into tin, level and bake for 30–35 minutes until well risen and firm. Leave in tin.

Gently heat caster sugar and lemon juice in small pan. Prick hot cake and spoon syrup over surface. Leave until cold and remove from tin.

For topping, heat lemon juice and gradually add to icing sugar until pouring consistency obtained. Add extra water or juice as required. Drizzle icing over cake and leave to set.

Scotch Chocolate Cake

From Bridgett L. Dickinson's grandmother on her father's side. My mom used to make this cake on Friday evenings, mixing the cake up while dinner was cooking and baking the cake while we ate. It is quick, easy, quite 'chocolatey', not fancy and tastes very good. Specially liked by children.

Mixing the cake

Combine the flour and sugar in a mixing bowl.

Put the butter, cocoa and water in a saucepan.

Melt the butter and bring to the boil, stirring the butter, cocoa, and water together.

Then pour the mixture over the flour and sugar and mix together.

Put the baking soda in the milk and add to the mixing bowl.

Mix together and add the eggs, and the vanilla.

Mix well and turn into a greased and floured pan about 23cm × 32cm (9" × 14").

Bake in the oven at 200°C/400°F/Gas Mark 6 for 30 minutes or until done.

Mixing the icing

Put the butter, milk, and cocoa in a saucepan and bring to a rapid boil, stirring constantly to prevent sticking.

Remove from heat and add the powdered sugar and vanilla, stirring thoroughly.

Put the icing on the cake 5 minutes before the cake is done and return to the oven for 5 minutes.

The icing is also good as a sauce: heat the icing mixture just before serving the cake. Serve the cake with ice cream and pour on the hot sauce.

For cake

2 cups 450g (16oz) unbleached white flour

2 cups 450g (16oz) sugar

1 stick unsalted butter (8 tbsp or 110g (4oz) butter)

4 heaped tbsp cocoa

1 cup water

$^1/_2$ cup buttermilk or $^1/_2$ cup milk with 1 tbsp white vinegar

1 tsp baking soda

2 eggs

1 tsp vanilla

For icing

1 stick butter (8 tbsp)

4 heaped tbsp cocoa

6 tbsp milk

1 half box (about 225g or 8oz) confectioner's sugar

(vary the sweetness and thickness by the amount of sugar added)

1 tsp vanilla flavoring

Supper Dishes

Tuna Supper Bake

This dish has 3 advantages:

1. *It can be made well in advance, and heated just before you want to eat.*
2. *It's a useful way of using up any kitchen leftovers: cooked sausages, bits of bacon, fried vegetables (especially red pepper), grilled or baked fish. It is particularly good with king prawns.*
3. *It's very tasty – and easily reheated the next day as well.*

Serves 2–3

350g (12oz) long grain rice

large can tuna fish in olive oil

half a cup of frozen peas

1 onion

110g (¼ lb) mushrooms (or more if you like), chopped

grated cheese for topping

White Sauce

50g (2oz) butter

25g (1oz) plain flour

275ml (½ pint) milk

Boil the rice by your preferred method until cooked (e.g. 2 cups rice to 1 cup water method, plus a saffron cube to colour the rice). When the water has boiled away, leave the rice in the saucepan with the lid on for 5–10 minutes to allow it to steam and soften.

Meanwhile, in a frying pan, heat a little oil and fry the onion, then add the mushrooms. This mixture should be thoroughly cooked. Cook the frozen peas gently.

Open the can of tuna, drain off the oil and place the tuna on a plate and break into flakes with a fork.

In an ovenproof casserole, put a layer of rice, then some peas, then some flaked tuna, then the onion and mushroom mix. End with a layer of rice.

Melt the butter in a saucepan, add the flour, then slowly add the milk to make a thick, plain white sauce. Pour over the rice mixture.

Finally, add the grated cheese on top and heat in a medium oven (180°C/350°F/Gas Mark 4) for 35–40 minutes. The cheese should be nice and crusty on top!

Serve with chutney and a green salad.

Cheeky Crispy Bacon with Cheesy Baked Potatoes

4 large potatoes

175g (6oz) mascarpone cheese

225g (8oz) bacon

175g (6oz) chestnut mushrooms, chopped

Serves 4

Spike the potatoes and butter their jackets. Bake them at 200°C/400°F/Gas Mark 6 for 1–1½ hours.

While potatoes are baking, grill bacon until crisp and break into pieces.

Cook mushrooms in olive oil until browned but still firm.

Cut open and spoon mascarpone cheese into potatoes, fluffing with a fork.

Add bacon and mushrooms on top.

Serve with green salad and a delicious glass of wine.

225g (8oz) shortcrust pastry

4 large eggs

3 tbsp milk

3 tbsp single cream

salt and pepper

pinch dried tarragon to taste

1 can asparagus spears

2 tbsp each of:
  shrimps
  diced bacon
  sweetcorn (canned)
  sliced mushrooms
  sliced tomatoes
  chopped onion
  sliced red pepper
  sliced green pepper

Cartwheel Quiche

Preheat oven to 190°C/375°F/Gas Mark 5.

Line a 25.5cm (10") flan dish with the pastry and bake for 10 minutes.

Sprinkle half the cheese over the base of the baked flan case.

Make a cartwheel with asparagus spears, placing a slice of tomato in centre.

Place shrimps, bacon, sweetcorn, mushrooms, tomatoes and onion in separate segments of the wheel.

Beat eggs, milk and cream together. Stir in tarragon and season with salt and pepper.

Pour over the other ingredients and sprinkle with rest of the grated cheese.

Return to oven for 25–35 minutes until egg is set and nicely browned.

Clodagh's Chilli

Serves 4

Fry the onion and garlic in the olive oil until the onions are transparent.

Reduce heat slightly; add the minced beef and brown very well, then reduce heat further.

Add the chopped tomatoes and tomato purée and mix well.

Add the chilli powder and the cumin, together with salt and black pepper to taste.

Add the peppers and the kidney beans and again, mix well.

(Add the celery and/or carrots at this stage if you use them.)

Cook for about 5 minutes.

Bring to the boil, stirring all the time.

Reduce to very low heat, cover and leave to simmer for about an hour.

Check on it once soon after you've reduced the heat to ensure it is not sticking or bubbling.

Serve in bowls. If desired, dollop some sour cream on top.

Accompany with a baked potato, or rice, or brown crusty bread.

A crisp, green salad is also a very refreshing addition.

---

2 tbsp olive oil

560g (1¼ lb) lean minced beef

2 onions, chopped

1 clove garlic, crushed

2 tbsp hot chilli powder (use more if you like a really hot chilli; this measure produces a fairly mild one, but with a little 'kick')

1 tsp ground cumin

400g (14oz) can chopped tomatoes

3 tbsp tomato purée

425g (15oz) can red kidney beans, rinsed

1 medium green or red pepper, deseeded and chopped

salt and black pepper to taste

2 sticks celery and/or 2 sticks carrots, chopped (optional)

Cornish Ham Pudding

Serves 2–3

6 slices white bread

40g (1½ oz) butter

3 slices ham

3 tomatoes

3 eggs

570ml (1pint) milk

salt and pepper

Remove crusts from bread and spread with butter.

Top with ham and then tomato slices. Cover with remainder of bread, buttered side up.

Cut into triangles and place in shallow buttered dish.

Beat eggs, salt and pepper and blend in milk. Pour over bread and garnish with tomato slices.

Bake in moderate oven for 35–45 minutes.

Hot 'n' Nutty Pasta

This makes quite a light meal or even a starter.

Serves 4

500g (1lb 2oz) shell pasta (more or less depending how hungry you are)

2 fresh green chillies, finely chopped

250g (9oz) walnuts, crushed

50g (2oz) fresh parsley, finely chopped

2 tbsp olive oil

Boil the pasta in the usual way.

Cook the chillies and the parsley for a couple of minutes in the olive oil and then add the pasta and the walnuts, mixing them up until the pasta is evenly coated in the oil and other ingredients.

Note For an altogether more substantial meal, fry 1 finely chopped onion and 2 crushed cloves of garlic and add to pasta along with a chopped-up can of anchovies and 110g (4oz) grated Parmesan cheese.

Meat Loaf

Sufficient for 2 × 450g (1 lb) loaf tins.

Preheat oven to 180°C/350°F/Gas Mark 5.

Put all ingredients (except eggs) in bowl and mix thoroughly. Stir in eggs.

Divide mixture into two greased 450g (1 lb) loaf tins and cook in the oven for 1 hour.

Ease the sides with a flat knife and turn out onto two plates.

Serve either hot with vegetables or cold with salad.

Freezes well.

900g (2 lb) minced beef

225g (8oz) sausagemeat

225g (8oz) fresh breadcrumbs

1 large onion, finely chopped

1 tbsp Worcester sauce

2 tsp ready-made mustard

3 eggs, beaten

2 tbsp tomato sauce

1 tsp dried mixed herbs

1 tbsp parsley

salt and pepper

Pasta with Roasted Red Peppers

Serves 4

Grill peppers under hot grill until the skin is blackened all over.

Wrap in clingfilm and leave to cool, then rub off skin under cold running water.

Cut peppers in half and remove seeds. Place peppers in food processor with mascarpone, garlic, herbs and olive oil. Mix together to make smooth sauce.

Cook pasta until tender, drain, return to pan and pour over sauce.

Serve with Parmesan and lashings of Chianti.

2 large whole red peppers, washed and dried

40g (1¹/₂ oz) mascarpone cheese or any soft full-fat cheese (such as Philadelphia)

3 cloves garlic, peeled (or to taste)

3 tbsp chopped fresh parsley

3 tbsp chopped fresh basil

3 tbsp olive oil

salt and black pepper

350g (12oz) dried pasta or 700g (1¹/₂ lb) fresh pasta

freshly grated Parmesan cheese to serve

Moussaka

Serves 3–4

225g (8oz) minced beef

1 onion

1 clove garlic

1 tbsp tomato purée

225g (8oz) can tomatoes

1 aubergine

2–3 potatoes, boiled in their skins, peeled and sliced

25g (1oz) butter

3–4 tbsp oil

salt and pepper

Béchamel Sauce

25g (1oz) butter

25g (1oz) plain flour

275ml (¹/₂ pint) milk

1 tsp mustard

1 egg, separated

50g (2oz) grated cheese

greaseproof paper

Melt butter, add chopped onion and garlic and minced beef and brown mixture.

Add tomato purée and tomatoes. Season. Simmer for ¹/₂–³/₄ hour.

Slice aubergine, sprinkle with salt and leave for ¹/₂ hour.

Béchamel Sauce

Melt butter, add flour and cook until granular. Add milk and cook until thickened. Beat in egg yolk, whip white until firm and add to sauce. Season. Cover with wet greaseproof paper until required.

Preheat oven to 200°C/400°F/Gas Mark 6.

Fry sliced aubergine in oil.

Arrange meat mixture, potatoes and aubergines in layers in ovenproof dish, starting with meat and finishing with aubergines.

Pour over sauce and brown in oven for 15 minutes.

Pizza

Preheat oven to 190°C/375°F/Gas Mark 5.

Knead together in a bowl the flour, baking powder, salt, margarine and milk.

To form the pizza base, roll out the dough mixture with rolling pin. Wet edges and fold in. Place on baking tray.

Spread tomatoes on base, followed by grated cheese, bacon, green pepper and onion.

Bake in oven for 15 minutes.

4 rounded tbsp flour
(2 wholemeal, 2 white)

1 tsp baking powder

pinch salt

25g (1oz) margarine

3 tbsp milk

2-3 peeled tomatoes

50g (2oz) grated cheese

1 rasher streaky bacon, chopped

green pepper, chopped

1/2 small onion, chopped

Rice and Crab Romanoff

Serves 6

Preheat oven to 180°C/350°F/Gas Mark 4.

Combine rice, chives, cottage cheese and mushrooms.

Blend natural yoghurt, mayonnaise, seasonings, Worcester sauce plus half the grated cheese.

Fold into rice mixture. Add crab meat (don't break lumps). Sprinkle with the remainder of the cheese and paprika.

Bake for 1/2 hour (covered).

Good with summer beans and cherry tomatoes.

3 cups hot cooked basmati rice

1/4 cup chives, chopped

1 cup creamed cottage cheese

1 can 110g (4oz) mushrooms, sliced

1/2 cup natural yoghurt

1/2 cup mayonnaise

3/4 tbsp salt

1/4 tsp each black and red pepper

1 tbsp Worcester sauce

1/4 cup grated Parmesan cheese

300g (11oz) lump crab meat

paprika

2 drops Tabasco sauce

Stuffed Sweet Peppers

Serves 4

350g (12oz) lean pork, coarsely minced

2 rashers bacon, diced

6 oz onion, finely chopped

4 well-shaped peppers (approximately 110g (4oz) each)

700g (1¹/₂ lb) tomatoes

50g (2oz) long grain rice

¹/₂ tsp granulated sugar

salt and pepper

oil or butter for frying

Preheat oven to 200°C/400°F/Gas Mark 6.

Wash peppers, cut a slice off from stem end (retaining these as lids) and remove core, seeds and thick pith.

Heat oil, fry half the onions until golden brown, add pork and bacon, and let this begin to change colour.

Wash and **parboil** rice (about 5 minutes), then drain and add rice to the pork and bacon mixture. Cook over a low heat for 10 minutes.

Meanwhile, peel and chop tomatoes and put them and remainder of onion into a small pan and cook until very soft. (If tomatoes are not juicy add 1–2 tbsp water.)

Add salt, pepper and sugar.

Put through a sieve or liquidize.

Arrange the peppers in a shallow oven dish, fill each with the fried mixture and replace tops.

Pour the sieved tomatoes round and bake for about 45 minutes or until the peppers are soft but still intact. If peppers become brown too early, cover with foil.

Spicy Prawn Risotto

Serves 2

Sauté the onion in the vegetable oil in a small frying pan until softened.

Add the mushrooms and tomatoes and continue cooking for a further 5 minutes.

Stir in the prawns, cooked rice, parsley, chilli powder and paprika.

Cook for 3–4 minutes more, stirring constantly.

Test for seasoning, adding salt and pepper and more chilli if preferred.

1 tsp vegetable oil
1 onion, finely chopped
175g (6oz) button mushrooms
400g (14oz) can chopped tomatoes
125g (4oz) frozen prawns (defrosted)
175g (6oz) cooked rice
4 tsp fresh parsley, chopped
2 tsp paprika
chilli powder to taste
salt and pepper

Tagliarini Sophia Loren

Courtesy of Giuliano's Ristorante, Edinburgh: this is their top-selling pasta dish, and is very popular in Italy.

Serves 2

Boil the pasta (this cooks very quickly) for about 3 minutes.

Fry the onions in a saucepan, then add all other ingredients except the pasta and Parmesan.

After this mixture has been cooking for a few minutes, add the pasta and Parmesan.

450g (1lb) fresh tagliarini pasta
110g (4oz) artichokes in oil, thinly sliced
110g (4oz) Parma ham, chopped
1 onion, chopped
110g (4oz) tomato sauce
150g (¼ pint) cream
2 tbsp Parmesan cheese, grated
parsley, chopped
crushed black pepper
salt

1 tbsp oil

200gm (7oz) tuna, drained

1 medium onion, chopped

1 clove of garlic, crushed

110g (4oz) mushrooms, sliced

1 can condensed mushroom soup

175g (6oz) pasta

110g (4oz) grated cheese (Cheddar or mozzarella)

50g (2oz) breadcrumbs

black pepper

Tuna with Pasta

Serves 3–4

Fry onion and garlic for 5 minutes until soft.

Add mushrooms and fry gently for another 2 minutes.

Add tuna, breaking it up roughly and mixing it with mushrooms and onions; add pepper to taste.

Stir in tin of mushroom soup and heat gently, do not boil – a little milk may need to be added at this stage.

Meanwhile prepare pasta according to instructions on packet.

Add cooked pasta to tuna mixture and turn into a large ovenproof dish.

Cover with mixture of grated cheese and breadcrumbs.

Grill until cheese is melted and breadcrumbs crispy.

Home Baking

Shortbread

Preheat oven to 180°C/350°F/Gas Mark 4.

Cream butter and sugar together, then mix in flour and cornflour.

Mix together until mixture resembles a ball of dough.

Press mixture into a baking tin – either oblong approximately 18cm × 28cm (7" × 11") or round approximately 18cm (7"). With a knife, mark out slices making a fairly deep impression – this helps to cut the shortbread after it has cooled. Then take a fork and prick the uncooked mixture well.

Place in the oven for 50–55 minutes.

When baked, leave shortbread in baking tin until cooled, then slice and place on cooling rack.

300g (10oz) plain flour

50g (2oz) cornflour

110g (4oz) caster sugar

225g (8oz) butter (good quality Danish is best)

Caramel Shortcake Squares

Preheat oven to 180°C/350°F/Gas Mark 4.

Cream butter with the sugar. Add flour and work to a smooth dough. Press into greased baking tin, 18cm × 28cm (7" × 11"). Bake for 20 minutes or until pale golden brown.

Melt all filling ingredients together and boil for 5 minutes, stirring all the time. Then beat for 2–3 minutes. The filling should be a pale fawn colour as the condensed milk caramelizes. Pour onto shortbread base and leave to cool.

Melt chocolate in a bowl over a pan of boiling water then pour onto filling. Leave to cool and cut into squares.

Base

110g (4oz) butter or margarine

50g (2oz) caster sugar

175g (6oz) plain flour

Filling

110g (4oz) butter or margarine

110g (4oz) caster sugar

1 small can condensed milk

4 level tsp syrup

Topping

175g (6oz) chocolate

Chocolate Cookies

This is a recipe from Abby Palmer's great-grandmother. She lived on the plains of the Mid-West and would start baking these cookies when she saw people at the end of the road coming for a visit. By the time they arrived, the cookies were coming out of the oven.

2 squares unsweetened chocolate

butter (size of an egg)

2 eggs

1 cup sugar

1 cup flour

$^1/_2$ tsp baking powder

Preheat oven to 150°C/300°F/Gas Mark 2.

Melt the chocolate and butter in a double boiler (bain-marie).

When melted, add 2 eggs – one at a time.

Beat in the sugar.

Mix in the flour and baking powder.

Put spoonfuls onto a greased baking tray.

Bake for 6–8 minutes.

110g (4oz) unsalted butter

75g (3oz) light brown sugar

75g (3oz) caster sugar

1 egg, beaten

125g (4$^1/_2$ oz) plain flour

$^1/_2$ tsp baking powder

200g (7oz) plain chocolate pieces

50g (2oz) chopped walnuts

Chocolate Chip Cookies

Makes 20

Preheat oven to 190°C/375°F/Gas Mark 5.

Mix together the butter and sugar until creamy and then stir in the beaten egg.

Fold the flour and baking powder into the creamed mixture. Add the chocolate and walnuts.

Place tablespoonfuls of the mixture onto lightly buttered trays and bake for about 10 minutes.

Quaker Oat Cookies

Preheat oven to 190°C/375°F/Gas Mark 5.

Melt the margarine and syrup in a small pan. Mix together the porridge oats, flour and sugar in a bowl before dissolving the baking soda in a small amount of warm water and adding to the bowl. Mix thoroughly. Add the melted margarine and syrup and mix it all together.

Roll into balls of about 2.5cm (1") and place on well-greased trays at least 5cm (2") apart.

Bake for 20 minutes. Place on wire racks to cool and harden.

110g (4oz) margarine

1 large tbsp syrup

110g (4oz) porridge oats (rolled oats not oatmeal)

110g (4oz) self-raising flour

110g (4oz) sugar

1 small tsp baking soda

Coconut Crisp Biscuits

Preheat oven to 180°C/350°F/Gas Mark 4.

Cream butter, brown sugar and granulated sugar till light and fluffy.

Beat in egg and vanilla essence.

Stir in flour, baking powder, bicarbonate of soda and salt.

Stir in cornflakes, coconut and chocolate drops.

Drop large teaspoonfuls onto baking tray and bake for 10–15 minutes.

110g (4oz) butter

75g (3oz) soft brown sugar

110g (4oz) granulated sugar

1 egg

1 tsp vanilla essence

150g (5oz) plain flour

1/2 tsp baking powder

1/2 tsp bicarbonate of soda

1/2 tsp salt

75g (3oz) cornflakes

75g (3oz) coconut

75g (3oz) chocolate drops

Anzac Biscuits

First made to commemorate the First World War Australian and New Zealand Armed Corps and, ever since, have traditionally been made on ANZAC Day (25 April).

100g (3½oz) unsalted butter

2 tsp golden syrup

2 tsp water

350g (12oz) rolled oats

200g (7oz) self-raising flour

125g (4½oz) sugar

1 tsp bicarbonate of soda

Preheat oven to 180°C/350°F/Gas Mark 4.

Melt butter, golden syrup and water in a saucepan.

Remove when cool and stir in oats, flour, sugar and bicarbonate of soda.

Roll into 3.5cm (1½") balls.

Gently flatten each ball onto a baking tray and cook for 30 minutes until golden brown.

175g (6oz) self-raising flour

75g (3oz) sugar

75g (3oz) margarine

1 egg, beaten

2 dsp coffee essence (Camp coffee)

Filling *(beaten together)*

110g (4oz) icing sugar

50g (2oz) margarine

a few drops of coffee essence

Coffee Kisses

Preheat oven to 180°C/350°F/Gas Mark 4.

Mix the flour and sugar and rub in the margarine.

Stir in the egg and coffee essence and mix well.

Form into balls the size of marbles (or bigger if desired).

Place on greased baking sheets and bake for about 15–20 minutes.

When cold, sandwich together in pairs with filling.

Grandma's Empire Biscuits

They're delicious – they just melt in your mouth.

Makes 12 complete biscuits

Preheat oven to 200°C/400°F/Gas Mark 6.

Cream together margarine and icing sugar until light and fluffy.

Add egg slowly, then sifted flour and custard powder. Using a metal spoon, fold in gently to make a stiff dough.

Knead lightly on a floured surface.

Wrap in greaseproof paper and leave in a cool place for 15 minutes.

Roll out to ½cm (¼") thickness and cut into small rounds. Place on a baking tray. Prick with a fork.

Bake on centre shelf for about 20 minutes or until golden brown. Spread on a wire tray to cool.

Sandwich together with jam, lemon curd or chocolate spread etc.

Tops can be iced and decorated for children's parties etc.

50g (2oz) soft margarine
50g (2oz) sifted icing sugar
1 small egg
150g (5oz) plain flour
25g (1oz) custard powder

Peanut Crunch Biscuits

Preheat oven to 180°C/350°F/Gas Mark 4.

Place peanuts, sugar, flour, salt and egg in a bowl.

Pour in melted margarine and mix well.

Place teaspoonfuls of mixture on greased tray.

Bake for 10 minutes.

1 cup raw peanuts
small cup sugar
1½ cups self-raising flour
110g (4oz) margarine, melted
1 egg
pinch salt

Milk Fudge

Makes about 50 pieces

300ml (¹/₂ pint) milk

800g (1lb 12oz) granulated sugar

100g (4oz) butter

2 tsp vanilla essence

Pour milk into pan. Bring slowly to the boil. Add sugar and butter.

Heat slowly, stirring all the time, until sugar dissolves and butter melts. Bring to the boil. Cover pan with lid. Boil for 2 minutes.

Uncover. Continue to boil steadily, stirring occasionally, for further 10–15 minutes (or until a little of the mixture, dropped into cup of cold water, forms soft ball when rolled gently between finger and thumb). Temperature on sugar thermometer, if used, should be 115–116°C/238–240°F.

Remove from heat. Stir in vanilla. Leave mixture to cool for 5 minutes.

Beat fudge until it just begins to lose its gloss and is thick and creamy.

Transfer to buttered 18cm (7") square tin. Mark into squares when cool.

Cut up with sharp knife when firm and set.

Store in airtight tin.

1 small can condensed milk

25g (1oz) margarine

25g (1oz) cocoa

2 tbsp coconut

10–12 digestive biscuits, crushed

chocolate vermicelli

Truffles

Melt margarine and condensed milk in a pan.

Take off the heat and add the coconut, cocoa and biscuits. Mix thoroughly.

Roll into small balls and coat with vermicelli.

Place in small paper cases.

Brandy Truffles

Boil the cream in a small heavy pan until reduced to 2 tablespoonfuls.

Remove from heat, stir in the alcohol and chocolate, and return to low heat; keep stirring until the chocolate melts.

Whisk in the softened butter.

When the mixture is smooth, pour onto a large plate and refrigerate until firm (about 1 hour).

Scoop the mixture up with a teaspoon and shape into truffle balls roughly 2.5cm (1") wide.

Roll the truffle balls in the cocoa powder, then place in truffle cases.

Store the truffles, covered, in the refrigerator. Let them stand at room temperature for about 20 minutes before serving.

4 tbsp double cream

2 tbsp Grand Marnier

175g (6oz) good quality chocolate, broken up

50g (2oz) unsalted butter, softened

powdered unsweetened cocoa

Variations

1. For Christmas truffles, sieve some icing sugar over the top for a 'snowy' effect.

2. Substitute the Grand Marnier with dark rum, cognac, Drambuie, Kahlua, Framboise, crème de menthe or amaretto.

Tablet

Boil milk and sugar for 10 minutes.

Add condensed milk and boil for another 10 minutes.

Take off heat and beat until mixture sets.

Place in baking tray and cut into shapes.

900g (2lb) sugar

1 large can condensed milk

1 cup milk

Granny Morrissey's Tea Cake

225g (8oz) self-raising flour

275g (10oz) sultanas

1 tsp mixed spice

110g (4oz) caster sugar

150ml (¼ pint) milk

110g (4oz) butter

2 eggs

Preheat oven to 170°C/325°F/Gas Mark 3.

Line a 20cm (8") cake tin with greaseproof paper.

Cream the butter and sugar.

Add flour, milk and eggs, and beat thoroughly.

Add the remaining ingredients.

Turn into cake tin and bake in the centre of the oven for 1½–1¾ hours.

Granny Morrissey's Christmas Cake

350g (¾ lb) butter

450g (1 lb) plain flour

110g (4oz) cherries

50g (2oz) ground almonds

225g (½ lb) seedless raisins

1 tsp mixed spice

grated rind of ½ lemon and juice

6 eggs

350g (¾ lb) caster sugar

110g (4oz) chopped peel

110g (4oz) chopped almonds

450g (1 lb) sultanas

225g (½ lb) currants

½ tsp nutmeg

2 tbsp golden syrup

1 glass rum (approximately a double measure)

Preheat oven to 140°C/275°F/Gas Mark 1.

Line a 23cm (9") cake tin with two layers of greaseproof paper.

Cream the butter and sugar in a mixer.

Add the eggs one at a time, and a little flour to prevent curdling, then the remainder of the flour.

Fold in all of the fruit and dry ingredients. Lastly add lemon juice, golden syrup and rum. Fold thoroughly.

Spoon the cake mixture into the tin. Bake for 6 hours. Remove from oven and leave to stand on a wire rack.

When cool, peel off the greaseproof paper and wrap in fresh greaseproof paper.

Ceylon Christmas Cake

Note Use a large mixing bowl (or a clean plastic washing up bowl) to allow for easy mixing.

Mix all the ingredients together. Put into a large airtight bottle or jar for 1–2 days. This will smell lovely when you start making the cake!

The day before you are ready to bake the cake, roast the semolina in a saucepan, **stirring all the time** until it is slightly brown. When cool, mix well with the butter and leave overnight.

Prepare 2 roasting tins with a few layers of good brown paper or greaseproof paper to prevent burning. The last layer should be well buttered (next to the cake).

Preheat oven to 140°C/275°F/Gas Mark 1.

Mix the caster sugar with the egg yolks until bubbly and creamy. Add the prepared butter and semolina mixture a tablespoonful at a time and beat until it too is creamy and bubbly.

Add the 'fruit mixture' a little at a time until well mixed, using a strong spoon in a very large bowl (a clean washing up bowl is ideal for this purpose).

Beat egg whites until stiff. Fold into the mixture.

Divide between the 2 roasting tins.

Cook one cake at a time for approximately 5 hours (test after 4 hours: as this is a very moist, rich cake, the skewer should not be bone dry).

Leave overnight until completely cool then wrap in foil. If desired, pour over a little more brandy before wrapping. Cake may also be covered with marzipan before serving.

350g (³/₄ lb) mixed candied peel

225g (¹/₂ lb) cashew nuts, finely chopped

450g (1 lb) ground almonds

450g (1 lb) raisins, chopped

450g (1 lb) glacé cherries, chopped

450g (1 lb) sultanas, chopped

450g (1 lb) pumpkin preserve

450g (1 lb) pineapple jam

450g (1 lb) ginger preserve

450g (1 lb) chow-chow (use marmalade)

4 tsp ground cardamoms

3 tsp ground cloves

1 tsp grated nutmeg

rind of 1 lemon, grated

150ml (5 fl oz) brandy

150ml (5 fl oz) rose water

150ml (5 fl oz) honey

3 tsp vanilla essence

1 tsp almond essence

Extra ingredients

450g (1 lb) semolina

900g (2 lb) caster sugar

25 egg yolks

10 egg whites

450g (1 lb) butter

Canadian Christmas Cake

200g (7oz) self-raising flour, sieved

¹/₄ tsp salt

150g (5oz) glacé cherries

450g (1 lb) canned pineapple, well-drained and finely chopped

150g (5oz) butter

110g (4oz) granulated sugar

2 large eggs

2 tbsp brandy

250g (9oz) sultanas

75g (3oz) cut mixed peel

Preheat oven to 160°C/325°F/Gas Mark 3.

Put flour and salt in a bowl.

Cut 8 cherries into small pieces and reserve.

Cut half of the remaining cherries into halves.

Roll the whole and halved cherries in the flour and shake off surplus.

Cream butter and sugar together, beat in eggs one at a time. Stir in flour, brandy and fruit.

Turn into a greased and lined 900g (2lb) loaf tin.

Level top and bake for ¹/₂ hour, then scatter reserved cherries over the top and continue to bake for another 1¹/₂–2 hours.

Leave until cool but not cold before turning out.

The cake should be left for at least a fortnight before cutting.

Wrap in foil if storing for any length of time.

2 large cooking apples, finely chopped

110g (4oz) butter

225g (8oz) plain flour

1 tsp baking powder

2 eggs

110g (4oz) sugar

2 tbsp milk

Knockroe Apple Cake

Preheat oven to 180°C/350°F/Gas Mark 4.

Line a 450g (1 lb) loaf tin with greasproof paper.

Cut butter into the flour and baking powder. Crumb together until the mixture resembles breadcrumbs.

Add sugar and apples, then pour in eggs and milk.

Put into the loaf tin and sprinkle sugar on top.

Bake for 40 minutes.

Carrot Cake

Preheat oven to 180°C/350°F/Gas Mark 4.

Grease and line a 20cm (8") cake tin.

Whisk egg yolks and sugar until thick and creamy.

Stir in carrots, almonds and lemon rind.

Whisk egg whites until stiff.

Fold in flour, then egg whites.

Pour into cake tin and bake for 40–45 minutes.

Serving suggestions

Serve either hot or cold with whipped cream or 50g (2oz) Philadelphia cheese and 25g (1oz) icing sugar mixed together.

3 eggs, separated
150g (5oz) soft brown sugar
225g (8oz) grated carrots
50g (2oz) ground almonds
75g (3oz) flaked almonds
50g (2oz) wholemeal flour
1 level tsp baking powder (sieved together)
grated rind of 1 lemon

Carrot Buns

Preheat oven to 180°C/350°F/Gas Mark 4.

Put sugar, margarine, mixed spice and flour into large mixing bowl, add beaten egg, then grated carrot. Beat well until mixture is soft and creamy.

Add sultanas, lemon juice and baking powder.

Put heaped teaspoonfuls into bun cases and bake for 20 minutes.

Cool on rack.

50g (2oz) soft brown sugar
75g (3oz) self-raising flour
1 small carrot, grated
1 tbsp lemon juice
1 level tsp mixed spice
50g (2oz) soft margarine
1 egg
1 tsp baking powder
1 tbsp sultanas

Apricot Tea Loaf

50g (2oz) dried apricots, chopped

150g (5oz) sultanas

250ml (¹/₂ pint) warm tea (brandy can be substituted for some of the tea if preferred)

110g (4oz) granulated sugar

1 egg

225g (8oz) self-raising flour, sieved

¹/₂ level tsp mixed spice

¹/₂ level tsp salt

Topping

1 rounded tbsp apricot jam

25g (1oz) sultanas

Place apricots and sultanas in mixing bowl, add tea and sugar, mix and leave to soak overnight.

Grease and line a 900g (2lb) loaf tin.

Preheat oven to 160°C/325°F/Gas Mark 3.

Stir egg into fruit mixture, sift flour, mixed spice and salt together, add to fruit and mix well.

Place in the loaf tin, levelling the top.

Bake in the centre of the oven for 1¹/₂ hours until well risen.

Leave in tin for 5–10 minutes, then turn out. Remove paper and allow to cool.

To make topping

Place apricot jam in pan over low heat and melt gently. Remove from heat and add sultanas.

Spread over tea loaf, cool and serve sliced and buttered.

Note Tea loaf will improve in flavour if stored in a tin. To freeze, wrap tea loaf, without topping, in foil or cling wrap.

---

1 cup (175g; 6oz) sultanas

1 cup (175g; 6oz) sugar

1 tsp bicarbonate of soda

1 tbsp treacle

1 egg

1 cup (220ml; 8 fl oz) water

110g (4oz) margarine

1 tsp mixed spice

2 cups (350g; 12oz) self-raising flour

Kilwinning Loaf

Preheat oven to 180°C/350°F/Gas Mark 4.

Grease a 450g (1 lb) loaf tin.

Put sultanas, water, sugar, margarine, bicarbonate of soda, mixed spice and treacle into saucepan and boil for 15 minutes.

Let the mixture cool slightly and add the flour and egg.

Turn into the loaf tin and bake for 45–55 minutes.

Malt Loaf

Preheat oven to 180°C/350°F/Gas Mark 3.

Grease and line a 900g (2lb) loaf tin.

Sift, flour, salt and bicarbonate of soda. Stir in sultanas. Warm malt and treacle together in pan until they become liquid and stir in milk and egg. Pour gently into dry ingredients and combine thoroughly.

Transfer to the loaf tin and bake for 30 minutes.

Reduce heat to 170°C/325°F/Gas Mark 3 and bake for further 15–20 minutes until springy to touch.

225g (8oz) self-raising flour

75g (3oz) sultanas

75g (3oz) malt extract

75g (3oz) black treacle

150ml (¼ pint) milk

1 egg, beaten

½ tsp salt

½ tsp bicarbonate of soda

Cranberry Nut Loaf

Preheat oven to 180°C/350°F/Gas Mark 4.

Grease a 23cm × 13cm (9" × 5") loaf tin.

Mix all the dry ingredients in the First section. Cut butter and crumb into the First section mixture.

Add the rest of the Second section ingredients to the First section ingredients and mix together.

The mixture should now be damp.

Fold the Third section ingredients into the mixture.

Spoon into the loaf tin, spreading corners and sides a little higher than the centre.

Bake until the crust is golden and a toothpick, when inserted, comes out clean and dry (about 1 hour).

Remove from tin and wait for one day before cutting.

First section

2 cups plain flour

2 tsp baking powder

1 tsp salt

1 cup caster sugar

½ tsp bread soda

Second section

¼ cup butter

¾ cup orange juice

1 tsp grated orange peel

1 egg, well beaten

Third section

½ cup walnuts, chopped

2 cups fresh cranberries, chopped

Banana Loaf

Preheat oven to 190–200°C/375–400°F/Gas Mark 5–6.

Rub flour and margarine together to the consistency of breadcrumbs. Add all other dry ingredients.

Mix in bananas and eggs.

Put into a greased and lined loaf tin and bake for about 1 hour 10 minutes.

Leave to cool in tin for a while, then turn out onto a wire rack.

Note Delicious spread with butter.

3 bananas, mashed

225g (8oz) brown self-raising flour

110g (4oz) margarine

75g (3oz) sugar

110g (4oz) sultanas

50g (2oz) dried apricots, chopped

1 egg

Nana's Fruit Tea Loaf

Preheat oven to 180°C/350°F/Gas Mark 4.

Grease and line a 450g (1lb) loaf tin.

Put the sugar, fruit and tea in a bowl and leave overnight. Add the egg and flour then mix all ingredients together.

Pour into the loaf tin and bake for 45 minutes.

1 cup (175g; 6oz) brown sugar

1 cup (175g; 6oz) sultanas and currants

1 cup (220ml; 8 fl oz) strong cold tea

1 egg, beaten

2 cups (350g; 12oz) self-raising flour

Treacle Loaf

Preheat oven to 170°C/325°F/Gas Mark 3.

Grease and line a 450g (1 lb) loaf tin.

Mix all ingredients together.

Pour mixture into the loaf tin and bake in the oven for ³/₄ hour.

2 cups (350g; 12oz) self-raising flour

1 cup (175g; 6oz) sugar (³/₄ brown, ¹/₄ white)

1 cup (175g; 6oz) mixed fruit

2 tbsp treacle

1 cup (220ml; 8 fl oz) milk

Banana Teabread

Preheat oven to 180°C/350°F/Gas Mark 4.

Grease and line a 23cm × 13cm (9"× 5") loaf tin.

Sift flour, soda and salt into a bowl.

Beat butter and sugar together in another large bowl until light and fluffy.

Add the eggs alternately with the flour.

Add the bananas to the mixture with any remaining flour, cherries and walnuts.

Spoon into loaf tin and bake for 1¼ hours.

Invert onto wire rack and cool.

225g (8oz) self-raising flour

¼ tsp bicarbonate of soda

½ tsp salt

75g (3oz) margarine

175g (6oz) caster sugar

2 eggs, beaten

3 bananas, mashed

50g (2oz) glacé cherries, chopped

50g (2oz) walnuts, chopped

Fluffy Banana Cake

Preheat oven to 180°C/350°F/Gas Mark 4.

Sieve all dry ingredients together into a bowl. Beat butter and sugar until creamy.

Add vanilla essence and eggs to the butter and sugar, and beat further.

Add bananas and milk. Mix until blended. Fold in dry ingredients.

Divide the mixture between two sandwich tins.

Bake in the oven for 30 minutes.

When cold, fill with whipped cream and mashed bananas.

Dust the top with icing sugar.

3 large bananas, mashed

½ tsp baking powder

½ tsp salt

275g (10oz) caster sugar

225g (8oz) plain flour

¾ tsp bread soda

110g (4oz) butter

2 eggs

2 tbsp sour milk

1 tsp vanilla essence

Filling

1 banana

150ml (¼ pint) cream, whipped

Banana Cake

150g (5oz) self-raising flour

¹/₄ tsp baking powder

1 ripe banana

50g (2oz) soft butter

1 egg

150g (5oz) caster sugar

¹/₂ tsp vanilla essence

1 tsp salt (optional)

Preheat oven to 190°C/375°F/Gas Mark 5.

Mash together banana, butter, egg, sugar, vanilla and salt, either by hand or in mixer.

Sieve flour and baking powder into mixture and mix well.

Spoon into a well-greased cake (or loaf) tin and bake for 40 minutes.

Note To use this as a dessert, omit the salt and bake in the cake tin, top with cream and decorate with sliced banana.

150g (5oz) carton of yoghurt (any flavour)

175g (6oz) butter, softened

110g (4oz) caster sugar

3 eggs

350g (12oz) self-raising flour

Yoghurt Cake

Serves 3–4

Preheat oven to 180°C/350°F/Gas Mark 4.

Grease an 18cm (7") round deep cake tin or two 18cm (7") sandwich tins.

Put all ingredients in bowl and beat together for 2–3 minutes.

Turn into tin or tins and bake for 45–55 minutes.

Serve the large cake as a cut cake or fill sandwich cakes with jam and butter icing.

The Best Chocolate Cake in the World

The members of the Marketing Department at Robert Stevenson House can attest to this claim. This is high in fat and low in fibre – and absolutely yummy!

Preheat oven to 180°C/350°F/Gas Mark 4.

Line base of 20cm (8") springform cake tin with greaseproof paper and grease sides lightly with knob of butter.

Melt 175g (6oz) chocolate over pan of water.

Cream 125g (4oz) butter and all the sugar in food processor, then add 4 egg yolks and whizz through.

Add ground almonds and whizz again. Turn out into a mixing bowl and add melted chocolate. Beat egg whites until stiff and fold in.

Pour into the cake tin and bake for 50–55 minutes until firm. Don't worry if the surface cracks.

Leave to cool then cover top with jam of choice.

Melt remaining butter and chocolate in a bowl over simmering water, stir well then spread over the top of the cake.

250g (9oz) plain, good-quality, cooking chocolate
175g (6oz) unsalted butter
125g (4oz) caster sugar
200g (8oz) ground almonds
4 large eggs, separated
as much as you want, best quality apricot or black cherry jam (use the really fruity variety, not cheap supermarket brand)

Snowballs

This is a good recipe for children to make for a school fair or fund-raising event.

Crush biscuits and add cocoa and coconut.

Mix in margarine and condensed milk.

Roll mixture round a mallow into a ball.

Roll in coconut and leave to set in the refrigerator.

50g (2oz) melted margarine
1 small can condensed milk
1 level tsp cocoa
50g (2oz) coconut
10 digestive biscuits
1 pkt marshmallows

Easy Sponge

110g (4oz) butter or margarine

110g (4oz) caster sugar

110g (4oz) plain flour

1 tsp baking powder

2 large eggs

Preheat oven to 170°C/325°F/Gas Mark 3.

Line 2 sandwich tins with greaseproof paper.

Sieve together all dry items then place all ingredients in a mixing bowl.

Beat with a wooden spoon for 2–3 minutes until light and fluffy.

Divide between two sandwich tins and bake for 30 minutes.

Sponge

85g (3¹/₂ oz) plain flour

1 level tbsp cocoa

¹/₂ level tsp bicarbonate of soda

¹/₂ level tsp baking powder

60g (2¹/₂ oz) caster sugar

1 tbsp golden syrup

1 egg

65ml (2¹/₂ fl oz) corn or vegetable oil

65ml (2¹/₂ fl oz) milk

Topping

3 tbsp rum

450g (1 lb) dark cooking chocolate

225g (¹/₂ lb) white cooking chocolate

275ml (¹/₂ pint) double cream

Light and Dark Cake

This family favourite is seriously fattening – great if you need cheering up, or just as a diet buster.

Preheat oven to 170°C/325°F/Gas Mark 3.

Mix together all sponge ingredients and place in a loose-bottomed cake tin 23cm (9") in diameter.

Cook until cake springs back when lightly pressed (approximately 25 minutes).

Allow sponge to cool, prick with skewer and sprinkle over rum. Press out of cake tin onto baking tray.

Whip cream until thick and set aside. Melt 225g (¹/₂ lb) dark chocolate in a bowl over hot water.

When chocolate has melted, fold into one-third of the cream. Pour over the sponge. Repeat above method with white chocolate, then repeat with remaining dark chocolate.

Note This cake is very sweet, so serve in small slices. It can be kept in the refrigerator if it's going to be eaten soon, or stored in the freezer and served frozen.

Lemon Sponge

Preheat oven to 170°C/325°F/Gas Mark 3.

Grease and line three 15cm (6–6½") sandwich tins.

Put all the ingredients into a mixing bowl and beat together with a wooden spoon or electric hand mixer. The mixture should drop easily from the spoon. Add a little milk if necessary.

Divide the mixture into the sandwich tins and bake on the middle shelf of the oven for 25–35 minutes. Cool on a wire rack.

Sandwich the layers with home-made lemon curd (see p. 189) and dust the top with icing sugar. For special occasions ice the top with lemon icing and decorate with mimosa balls or real flowers, e.g. freesias.

175g (6oz) margarine (Blue Band is recommended)

175g (6oz) caster sugar

3 large eggs

175g (6oz) self-raising flour, sifted

1½ level tsp baking powder

Blueberry Muffins

Makes 12

Preheat oven to 180°C/350°F/Gas Mark 4.

Grease 12 deep bun tins.

Sift the flour, sugar and baking powder into a bowl.

Stir in the egg, butter and milk.

Fold in the blueberries.

When the mixture resembles a thick batter, divide the mixture into the tins.

Bake for 20 minutes. Best eaten warm.

250g (9oz) plain flour

100g (4oz) caster sugar

3 tsp baking powder

1 egg

50g (2oz) unsalted butter, melted

250ml (½–¾ pint) milk

125g (4½ oz) blueberries

Fluffy Pancakes

2 cups (350g; 12oz) plain flour

1 tsp cream of tartar

1 tsp baking soda

1 tbsp melted margarine

1 egg

1 cup (220ml; 8 fl oz) milk

2 tbsp sugar

First, melt the margarine, then beat the sugar and egg together and add the melted margarine. Dissolve the baking soda in a cup of milk and pour in with the margarine, sugar and egg mixture. Mix the cream of tartar with the flour and add to create a batter. Beat thoroughly.

Grease and heat a large flat pan (frying pan or pancake griddle), preferably a thick-bottomed one. Using a dessertspoon or tablespoon (depending upon the size of pancake you require), spoon the batter on to the frying pan two or three pancakes at a time. Once bubbles start appearing on the top surface (not just at the edges), the pancake is ready to be flipped over. Cook the other side and serve hot.

For a Scottish flavour, make small pancakes and serve with raspberry jam and whipped cream, or make a full-size Canadian-style pancake and serve with bacon, sausages and maple syrup.

Note These pancakes are quite thick and fluffy, unlike French crêpes.

110g (4oz) treacle

110g (4oz) syrup

225g (8oz) margarine

225g (8oz) soft brown sugar

350g (12oz) plain flour

$1/4$ tsp salt

2 level tsp ground ginger

1 tsp cinnamon

2 eggs

150ml ($1/4$ pint) milk

2 level tsp baking soda

Gingerbread

Preheat oven to 170°C/325°F/Gas Mark 3.

Melt sugar, syrup, treacle and margarine over gentle heat.

Sift dry ingredients except baking soda and add to melted mixture.

Add beaten eggs and milk heated with baking soda.

Bake for 1–1$1/2$ hours.

Granny's Country Scones

Preheat oven to 190°C/375°F/Gas Mark 5.

Mix together all dry ingredients. Add margarine and stir in sultanas. Bind to a softish dough with beaten egg and milk.

Roll out onto a floured surface and using a scone cutter cut out scones. Brush tops with beaten egg.

Bake for 15 minutes

Alternatives

1. Glacé cherries may be used instead of sultanas but omit mixed spice.
2. Omit sugar and spices and replace sultanas with 3oz grated Cheddar cheese then sprinkle more cheese over top before baking.

275g (10oz) wholewheat flour
75g (3oz) soft margarine
1tsp baking powder
large pinch of salt
50g (2oz) sugar
1 heaped tsp mixed spice
150g (5oz) sultanas
1 large egg, beaten
3 tbsp milk

Oven Scones

Preheat oven to 200°C/400°F/Gas Mark 6.

Sift flour and salt into a bowl. Rub in butter until mixture has the consistency of breadcrumbs.

Add sugar and baking powder. Beat egg in a teacup and add milk until volume is about half a cup. Add this to the flour (reserving a little for brushing tops) and mix together.

Turn out on to a floured board and knead lightly. Roll out and cut into scone shapes.

Brush the tops with a little reserved beaten egg/milk.

Bake for about 10 minutes.

110g (4oz) plain flour
pinch of salt
10g ($\frac{1}{2}$ oz) butter
10g ($\frac{1}{2}$ oz) caster sugar
$\frac{1}{2}$ tsp baking powder
1 egg
milk

Olive Oil and Fennel Breadsticks

These breadsticks make an ideal hostess gift, wrapped in a cloth napkin and presented on a dish or in a basket.

Makes 48 sticks

Note *1 cup = 225g (8oz)*

³/₄ cup warm water
(105–115°F)

³/₄ cup warm beer
(105–115°F)

1 pkt dry yeast

³/₄ cup olive oil

1 tbsp fennel seeds

1¹/₂ tsp salt

4¹/₂ cups all-purpose
flour

non-stick vegetable
oil spray

1 egg, beaten with
1 tbsp water

Place water and beer in a large bowl; sprinkle yeast over and stir to dissolve. Allow to stand for 10 minutes. Add oil, fennel seeds and salt. Mix in 3¹/₂ cups flour.

Knead dough on floured surface until smooth and elastic, adding more flour by the tablespoon if sticky (about 8 minutes if kneaded by hand; less if a machine is used). Place dough in a large bowl and cover with cling wrap. Allow to rise in a warm place until doubled in volume (1–2 hours, depending on temperature).

Preheat oven to 180°C/350°F/Gas Mark 4. Spray baking sheets with oil. Punch dough down. Divide into 12 balls. Cut each ball into quarters. Roll out each piece (between palms or against a flat surface) into a 30cm (12") long 'snake' and place on baking sheet. Brush with egg mixture. Bake for about 35 minutes, or until brown. Cool slightly before moving.

Optional Sesame seeds, coarse salt or crushed rosemary leaves may be sprinkled over the egg-glazed dough before baking for a different flavour.

Brown Bran Bread

Preheat oven to 180°C/350°F/Gas Mark 4.

Combine all ingredients except the buttermilk.

Make a well in the centre of the mixture and add the milk, holding back some in case it is too wet.

Mix with a wooden spoon until it all sticks together. Knead and form a ball.

When the dough is firm enough to pick up in one piece, put it in a loaf tin and bake in the centre of the oven for 45–50 minutes.

Remove from tin and wrap in a clean tea towel.

Stand it upright against the wall until it cools.

---

3 mugs good-quality brown flour

1 mug plain white flour

1½ tsp salt

half mug wheatgerm

1½ tsp bread soda

⅓ mug bran

570ml (a generous pint) buttermilk

Highland Wheaten Bread

Preheat oven to 160°C/325°F/Gas Mark 3.

Grease a 900g (2lb) loaf tin.

Put the flours, oats, salt and sugar in a bowl. Sift in the baking soda to make sure there are no lumps. Make a well in the centre and pour in all the liquid. Mix thoroughly with a wooden spoon until no dry flour remains.

Put into the loaf tin and bake for 1¼ hours.

Using a knife, check to see if it is cooked: insert into the thickest part of the bread and if it comes out clean the bread is cooked. Allow to cool in the tin for 15 minutes, then remove to a wire rack. This bread keeps moist for several days.

450g (1lb) stoneground wholemeal flour

15ml (3 tsp) baking soda

1 rounded tsp salt

15ml (1 tbsp) sugar (or diabetic alternative)

110g (4oz) porridge oats

50g (2oz) white self-raising flour

2 eggs, beaten

570ml (1 pint) buttermilk or 150ml (¼ pint) yoghurt and 425ml (¾ pint) water

Butteries

Preheat oven to 220°C/425°F/Gas Mark 7.

Make up dried yeast as per packet instructions with the tepid water, then add sugar.

Mix with flour to an elastic dough. Let it stand near heat or in hot water tank cupboard for 1 hour.

Mix lard and salt well and divide into 3 parts.

Roll out dough and spread with 1 part lard over dough. Fold in 3 and roll out. Roll and fold twice more with the lard.

At end of rolling finish up with a square.

Cut into 12–15 pieces. Keep warm for 30 minutes.

Put small knobs of margarine on top of each piece.

Bake until golden brown.

3 cups plain flour

3 level tsp salt

110g (4oz) lard

self-raising flour
(for rolling out)

3 tsp sugar

10g (¹/₂oz) pkt dried
yeast

1¹/₂ cups tepid water

margarine for topping

350g (12oz) fine oatmeal

110g (4oz) plain flour

110g (4oz) lard

1 cup cold water

1 tsp salt

1 tsp baking powder

¹/₂ tsp bicarbonate of
soda

1 tbsp sugar

Oatcakes

Makes 32

Preheat oven to 200°C/400°F/Gas Mark 6.

Mix all dry ingredients in a bowl and rub in the lard.

Mix with enough water to form very soft mixture.

Divide into 85g (3–4oz) balls and roll out onto floured surface in a circle.

Cut into four. Do not grease trays.

Cook for approximately 20 minutes.

Finishing Touches

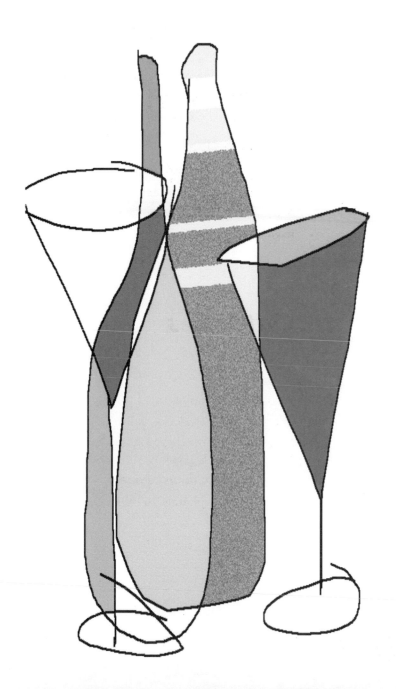

Lemon Curd

A delicious alternative to jam.

Melt butter in pan but do not let it go brown.

Add sugar, lemon rind and juice.

Stir over low heat until sugar melts but do not boil.

Remove from heat and add beaten eggs.

Put back on heat and stir until bubbling.

Remove from heat and pour into a jar.

2 eggs
2 lemons
2 cups sugar
1 small piece of butter (size of a walnut)

Hot Cherry and Chocolate Sauce

Ideal sauce for ice cream.

Serves 4

Strain cherries.

Put the syrup into a pan and heat gently. Add cherry brandy liqueur.

Blend the arrowroot into 4 teaspoonfuls of cold water and add this to the syrup mixture.

Stir in the cherries.

Grate a little dark chocolate on top and serve immediately.

1 can cherries in syrup
75ml (3 fl oz) cherry brandy liqueur
2 tsp arrowroot
dark chocolate, grated for decoration

Damson Gin

Delicious as an aperitif.

Makes about 1¹/₂ bottles

1.1kg (2¹/₂ lb) damsons

450g (1lb) sugar

1 bottle gin

Prick the fruit and place in a bowl (or a large, used, ice cream container with lid is ideal).

Add the sugar and gin, stir. Cover the bowl and leave aside. Stir once a day for the following 6 weeks.

When ready, strain and bottle.

2 measures Tequila (half a standard bottle)

1 measure Cointreau (quarter of a bottle or less, to taste)

2 measures lime (one bottle Jiff lime and a few peeled fresh limes thrown in)

Margarita

Serves 6–8

Mix the ingredients in a jug with lots of ice and leave until the ice starts to dilute the ingredients. Place some lime juice on the rim of the glasses and dip into some salt.

Garnish with fresh lime.

1 measure bacardi (half a 75 cl bottle)

1 measure pineapple juice (500ml)

1 measure creamed coconut (one 400g can)

Pina Colada

Mix the ingredients in a large jug.

Liquidize with a hand blender if necessary as the coconut can be lumpy.

Add lots of ice just before serving and garnish with a slice of pineapple.

1 teacup whisky

1 large can condensed milk

3 eggs

2 dsp coffee essence (Camp coffee)

2 tsp vanilla essence

Whisky Cream Drink

Place all the ingredients in a blender and whisk for approximately 1 minute.

When thoroughly mixed, bottle and chill before serving.

Keeps well.

Bacon and Tomato Sauce

(to accompany pasta shapes)

Serves 4

Fry onion, garlic and bacon until soft.

Add celery and carrots, and fry for 2 minutes, stirring continuously.

Add at least a tablespoonful of tomato purée, stir well and add the tomatoes.

Top up with cider and season.

Cook for at least 30 minutes with lid on.

Note Wine can be used instead of cider and fresh tomatoes instead of canned.

5–6 thick rashers of bacon, cut into small squares

1 onion, chopped

2 sticks of celery, chopped into small chunks

2 carrots, finely grated

cider

oil (olive oil is recommended)

salt and pepper

tomato purée

425g (15oz) can chopped tomatoes

garlic/garlic purée

oregano

Barbeque Sauce for Basting Meats

Mix mustard and cornflour in a saucepan and gradually blend in stock.

Add other ingredients, place over heat and bring to the boil, stirring all the time.

Simmer for a few minutes until blended.

Cool and use to baste beef, lamb, chicken or pork for the barbeque.

1 tbsp dry mustard

1 tbsp cornflour

275ml (1/2 pint) chicken stock

4 tbsp tomato ketchup

2 tbsp Worcester sauce

50g (2oz) brown sugar

salt

paprika

Cranberry Sauce

Delicious served with turkey, chicken, pork or ham.

450g (1lb) cranberries

zest and juice of an orange

1 cinnamon stick

75g (3oz) sugar

2 tbsp port

Put all ingredients into a pot and slowly bring to the boil.

Reduce heat and simmer for 5 minutes.

Remove cinnamon stick and pour into small jars.

When cold, seal and store in refrigerator until required.

Dill and Mustard Sauce

Serve with smoked salmon.

150ml (¼ pint) mayonnaise

1 tbsp Dijon mustard

1 tbsp clear honey

2 tsp soy sauce

white pepper

2 tsp dill, chopped

Stir all ingredients together in a bowl.

Cover and leave in refrigerator for several hours for flavours to mix.

Pesto Sauce

3 packed cups fresh basil

4 large cloves garlic

⅓ cup toasted pine nuts (optional)

⅓ cup olive oil

⅓ cup grated Parmesan cheese

salt and pepper to taste

Mince the basil and the garlic in a blender or food processor.

Add the pine nuts and blend until finely ground.

Keep the machine running and drizzle in the olive oil.

When you have a smooth paste, transfer the mixture to a bowl, stir in Parmesan and season with salt and pepper.

Green Tomato Chutney

This is Andrew Stevenson's mother-in-law's famous chutney, consumption of which guarantees perpetual youth, wealth, happiness – and hunger for more chutney.

Peel and cut up the tomatoes. Peel, core and cut up the apples. Chop the garlic.

Using a rolling pin, crush the ginger and put in a muslin bag together with the chillies.

Boil all ingredients together for about an hour until it thickens.

Fill jars and when completely cold, put lids on and store.

Makes about 2 kg 700g (6lb). Keeps for at least 2 years.

1kg 800g (4lb) green tomatoes
900g (2lb) cooking apples
450g (1lb) sultanas
110g (^{1}/$_4$lb) salt
75g (3oz) dried root ginger
10g (^{1}/$_2$ oz) dried chillies
900g (2lb) demerara sugar
50g (2oz) garlic
2 quarts (4 pints) vinegar
110g (4oz) mustard seeds, soaked overnight

Quantities are rather arbitrary as it depends how much you want to make but match the weight of tomatoes with the weight of onions.

green tomatoes, sliced

onions, sliced

green peppercorns, crushed

pickling vinegar

olive oil

sterile Kilner jars

Green Tomato Pickle

This is an excellent recipe if you grow tomatoes and don't know what to do with unripe ones that drop off the vine. You can sometimes buy them but as an alternative use cucumbers, courgettes or a mix of peppers.

Heat the vinegar to boiling point.

Using a metal sieve, lower the tomatoes and onions into the boiling vinegar a few slices at a time. Keep them under the surface for about 30 seconds or until they are parboiled and a little soft.

When all the onions/tomatoes have been in the vinegar begin the layering in the Kilner jars: start off with a layer of tomatoes, then onions, then sprinkle on some crushed pepper and pour oil over the layers. Repeat this process until the jar is fully layered with onions and tomatoes and the oil reaches the brim.

Seal the jar (airtight if possible – most Kilner jars come with instructions) and leave the pickle to steep for several weeks/months/years or until you want to use.

Index

Index

Notes

Notes

Notes

Notes

Notes

Notes

Notes

Notes

Notes

Notes